Sandspurs

The Florida History and Culture Series

Florida A&M University, Tallahassee
Florida Atlantic University, Boca Raton
Florida Gulf Coast University, Ft. Myers
Florida International University, Miami
Florida State University, Tallahassee
New College of Florida, Sarasota
University of Central Florida, Orlando
University of Florida, Gainesville
University of North Florida, Jacksonville
University of South Florida, Tampa
University of West Florida, Pensacola

Sandspurs

Notes from a Coastal Columnist

Mark Lane

Foreword by Raymond Arsenault and Gary R. Mormino

University Press of Florida

Gainesville · Tallahassee · Tampa · Boca Raton · Pensacola
Orlando · Miami · Jacksonville · Ft. Myers · Sarasota

13 12 11 10 09 08   6 5 4 3 2 1

Library of Congress Cataloging-in-Publication Data
Lane, Mark, 1956–
Sandspurs: notes from a coastal columnist/Mark Lane;
foreword by Gary R. Mormino and Raymond Arsenault.
p. cm.—(The Florida history and culture series)
Includes index.
ISBN 978-0-8130-3234-4 (alk. paper)
I. Title.
PN4874.L235A25 2008
814.'69–dc22   2008002687

The University Press of Florida is the scholarly publishing
agency for the State University System of Florida, comprising
Florida A&M University, Florida Atlantic University, Florida
Gulf Coast University, Florida International University, Florida
State University, New College of Florida, University of Central
Florida, University of Florida, University of North Florida,
University of South Florida, and University of West Florida.

University Press of Florida
15 Northwest 15th Street
Gainesville, FL 32611-2079
http://www.upf.com

For the guys, Rachel and Nathan

Contents

Foreword

Sandspurs: Notes from a Coastal Columnist is the latest volume in a series devoted to the study of Florida history and culture. During the past half-century, the burgeoning population and increased national and international visibility of Florida have sparked a great deal of popular interest in the state's past, present, and future. As a favorite destination of countless tourists and as the new home for millions of retirees and transplants, modern Florida has become a demographic, political, and cultural bellwether. Florida has also emerged as a popular subject and setting for scholars and writers. The Florida History and Culture Series provides an attractive and accessible format for Florida-related books. From killer hurricanes to disputed elections, from tales of the Everglades to profiles of Sunbelt cities, Florida is simply irresistible.

The University Press of Florida is committed to the creation of an eclectic but carefully crafted set of books that will provide the field of Florida studies with a new focus to encourage Florida writers to consider the broader implications and context of their work. The series includes standard academic monographs as well as works of synthesis, memoirs, and anthologies. And, while the series features books of historical interest, authors researching Florida's environment, politics, literature, and popular or material culture are encouraged to submit their manuscripts as well. Each book offers a distinct personality and voice, but the ultimate goal of the series is to foster a broad sense of community and collaboration among Florida scholars.

Mark Lane is a Florida original. A journalist for the *Daytona Beach News-Journal* since 1980, Lane has established himself as one of the state's most gifted columnists. Now Floridians and non-Floridians can appreciate his droll sense of humor and wry insights. In *Sandspurs: Notes from a Coastal Columnist* Lane alternates between a cynicism borne of a career observing fast-talking lawyers and slow-witted politicians trying to bulldoze Volusia County and a fierce defensiveness toward newcomers and outsiders who ridicule Florida and aim to sweep away the alligator farms while complaining that Florida has no culture.

Lane's essays on sharks, wild fires, and Sunshine State Noir deserve a wide readership. "Only in Florida do political wonks write crime novels," he writes, asking, "In how many other states would a political comptroller be fodder for fiction?" He quotes a New Yorker, wandering into a 2004 hurricane party bar, exclaiming, "This is better than Disney World!" After surviving Hurricanes Charley and Frances, he proposes a new idea for an optimist: "Somebody who takes down his plywood." Lane's pet peeves include "smart growth" disciples, specialty license plates, bump drafters, and the Army Corps of Engineers.

Expressing an unabashed fondness for a vanishing Florida and Volusia County, Lane regrets the loss of hammock and wetlands, but also the endangered "funky beachside." He fulminates, "We have environmental preservation zones. We have historic sites. But who's looking out for the low-rent beachside [as in Beverly Beach in Flagler County]?"

Raymond Arsenault and Gary R. Mormino
Series coeditors

Preface

For a newspaper columnist, Florida is as close as it gets to a workers' paradise. Yeah, I know, all columnists like to think they live in places that are amazing once you get to know them. The implied social contract between metro columnist and reader is that if you'll give him your time, the columnist will show you how remarkable things are—once you get below the surface.

In Florida no such qualification is needed. We stare out the window and type. Here, the social contract between metro columnist and reader requires only that you, the reader, walk away weirded out on occasion.

For here the politics are stranger, the crime more outrageous, and the intersection of the two more frequent than is considered strictly normal in a modern industrialized democratic republic. Even nature and the elements are over-the-top. And then there's this land rush that has been going on since the end of World War I, pausing only occasionally when recessions let everyone catch their breath. The economic history of the past one hundred years reads like slapstick. So columnists who set up shop in Florida need only convince you that they're not making anything up.

Where columnists in other places write about their surroundings to impart a warm feeling of shared recognition, a Florida columnist races to get things down before they disappear and the casual reader no longer has any idea what he's talking about. Sometimes I find myself writing about the landscape of the 1980s as though it were a lost world.

There are so many new people showing up between editions that I can be fairly useful to readers doing nothing more than explaining why basic stuff is the way it is. In a state with a political memory measured in months, the guy who can remember five years back is a sage. To talk about ten years back is to transmit half-disbelieved lore about the Time of the Ancient Ones.

I came to Daytona Beach, Florida, the World's Most Famous Beach, in 1961 when my parents drove my sister and me down U.S. Highway 1 in the back of an AMC Rambler American station wagon. We were part of the

New Frontier's Great Florida Aerospace Migration, a population movement that still figures in the state mythos.

My parents still live in the white concrete-block house we pulled up to, the one with the big magnolia tree. And I still work for the paper that was on our driveway in the morning, in the newsroom where I worked when I was in high school.

That is a lot of stay-putness in a state as hypermobile as Florida. It seems almost un-American. But I have been unsuccessful at imagining myself into anywhere else. To paraphrase Henry David Thoreau, I have traveled much in Volusia County.

These are columns that grew out of that background. They all first appeared in the *Daytona Beach News-Journal*, where I have been writing in some capacity since 1980.

The *News-Journal* is one of the nation's few locally owned daily newspapers. This setup frees me from corporate second-guessing from people who don't know me in out-of-state offices I'm not aware of. And I have been free to be three kinds of columnist: a humor columnist, a political columnist, and a regional color columnist. Four, if you count a garden columnist of a specialized kind. I drive to work each morning never knowing which one I'll be.

The columns selected here are, to varying degrees, attempts to explain the state to people. An easy sell in a state with a fluid identity. A state where a popular pastime is talking about where to move next—the locals because the changes, growth, buildup, and landscape destruction are breaking their hearts; the newcomers because this was not at all what they had imagined. A surprising percentage of people seem to be reevaluating the place week to week. And I suspect this makes us more aware of our surroundings than people elsewhere.

Many parts of the country have their identity all worked out. If you're a Hoosier or if you're from Down East or the Deep South, you have a stockpile of a century or two of stock types, familiar jokes, and regionalisms to bring to the show. Here we're still making all that up.

This means that the Great Florida Myth is still fuzzy, and so my guesses at its particulars are as good as anybody's and easily revised in next week's editions. Many celebrated early attempts to come up with something along these lines simply unpacked cultural baggage from elsewhere, mostly the rest of the South. The results often had nothing to do with the place.

If you look at the pediment of the old Florida Capitol in Tallahassee, you'll see a scene that was supposed to embody the spiritual mythology of this place. Little about it seems to be from around here. There are *mountains* in the background. Yeah, mountains in Florida. Think about that: until 1978, people were writing our laws in a building that depicted the place as a mountainous fairyland. This probably explains a lot of our political history.

An ongoing search for the not-yet-solidified Great Florida Myth is as close as you'll get to a theme in this book, but I'm not making promises. All this is deadline work, cleaned up for company. Read it fast while it still makes sense.

Acknowledgments

Neither my column nor this book could have come about without the support, forbearance, and suspension of disbelief by the staff and management of the *Daytona Beach News-Journal*. In particular, its editor, Don Lindley, and Herbert M. "Tippen" Davidson Jr., CEO until his death in 2007, and Josephine Davidson, his late wife. Also John Carter, metro columnist until his death in 2000.

I'd be remiss if I didn't also thank Kay Semion, Krys Fluker, Bruce Beattie, Ana deLane and Lindor Reynolds. Finally, thanks to my children, Rachel and Nathan Lane, who not always knowingly contributed much material over the years, and my parents, John and June Lane.

1 Hurricane season

"Living without electricity for five days isn't
so bad. It's like camping, except you know
where your stuff is."

—*The Darwinian Gardener's Almanac*

Illustration by Bruce Beattie.

Storm watchers out in force for Irene

"There goes your awning, Tony!" somebody shouted from the back of the Pit Stop Pub. The awning had ripped loose and was twisting in the air above the Boardwalk. A dragging sound came from overhead as it landed on the roof. This was the outer edge of Hurricane Irene and the winds were gusting in the 40–50 mph range.

"Sounds like you got your awning back," another voice shouted.

The "Mike Shallow for City Commission" sign flew off a few minutes later.

About twenty people were in the bar Saturday. A good-sized group for the middle of a hurricane. The television on the wall alternated between the Alabama-Mississippi game and a green map of Florida with swirls of nasty color east of Daytona Beach.

"You should have been here earlier. There were more people here a few hours ago," said the owner, Tony Mozz.

It is probably bad storm-preparedness to be watching tidal surges from a bar overlooking the beach, but Mozz says storm-watching in his place has become something of a regular event, particularly during this active season of storms. As he spoke, the television competed with the steady whine of the wind. Outside, concrete benches tipped over, palms bent into graceful arcs, and the surf lapped halfway up the steps between Boardwalk and beach.

Hurricane Irene was quite a show, and to the group nestled in the pub at the base of Main Street Pier—the same pier that had lost three hundred feet to Hurricane Floyd—it felt like being in a skybox. The group whooped each time the electricity flickered. When the door swung open, each customer was announced with a roar of wind and a blast of rain.

"Did you see that awning go?" asked a woman who walked in.

She was soaked to the skin and gripped a soggy disposable camera. She and her husband were visiting from upstate New York. The storm had stranded them in town, and they were more than making the best of it. "This is better than Disney World!" she declared. Her husband agreed.

I agreed. A huge, churning surf accompanied by a wind that could knock you on your back, this was something awesome. Even at its peak danger, the spectacle beckoned sightseers. Earlier, in the parking lot near the Bandshell, I saw seven cars parked in a line, their occupants watching the sea as if it were a drive-in movie. When a surge splashed over the sea wall in front of them, four cars prudently took off for higher ground. The rest stayed put.

Several yards out to sea, the waves tossed a surfboard into the air, fins up. I squinted into the ocean spray and looked for the surfer. He had regained his board and was trying again. You may wonder why someone would attempt something as contrary to normal self-preservation instincts as surfing in a hurricane. I don't know, either. That's why I made my way to the beach. I thought I'd ask him. The wind and current, however, swept him south fast, and I lost sight of him. Which was how I ended up at the Pit Stop Pub.

"I expect he's at Ponce Inlet by now," said the waitress.

"Now that's dumb," commented the big, thirtyish guy in a palm-tree print shirt standing next to me who said his name was Sean.

He said he lives nearby and got tired of sitting inside listening to things bumping around, so he strolled into the storm. He had walked more than a mile and was drying out in the bar, where he declared the whole thing to be a hoot and an excellent minor adventure. On the walk back he amused himself by spreading out his arms and seeing how far forward and at what kind of angle he could lean into the wind.

"This is great!" he shouted, almost drowned out by the surf and the wind gusts.

Doing this was very dumb and under easily imaginable circumstances might even kill you, but, yeah, it was hard not to share his exhilaration. Nor was he a rarity. All along the coast people were drawn to the edge of an angry sea. They ranged from the heedless surf dude and the tattooed teenager sighted in the waves near the pier to those more cautiously parked and watching the surf while dry in their cars.

One of the odder effects of this year's string of hurricanes is the way the whole hurricane drill seems more routine. Just another part of life in Florida. A show for the tourists; a diversion for the locals. And heck, the bad part of the storm is way out over the horizon somewhere.

And it would take something very terrible to keep these folks away next time.

October 1999

Postscript: The Pit Stop Pub was torn down in 2004. A loss to the community, reporters, and out-of-town TV-news crews.

It takes a storm to clear a garage

Hurricane season starts today, which makes this the traditional week for storm-preparedness lectures. Polls suggest the majority of Floridians have already put the overactive 2004 hurricane season so very far behind them, they only vaguely recall the fuss. This is not without positive effects—both psychological and economic. The current real estate boom could not have happened without a sustained, large-scale effort at group forgetting. Congratulations to everyone involved.

Though this exercise in group amnesia is an excellent thing for home values and the state's general sense of well-being, it does make for poor storm preparedness. I, for one, still have no idea where any flashlight is in my house. And I think most people with children would have to admit the same. The flashlights that the kids haven't walked off with are the ones I've hidden so well that I cannot find them.

The state of Florida is trying to nudge us into better storm preparedness with a sales-tax holiday for hurricane supplies. A nice idea, and I intend to buy enough batteries to fill all my missing flashlights. Still, it's unfortunate that one of the most important acts of hurricane preparedness isn't helped a bit by the sales-tax holiday. And when the storm advisories are issued for real, it's almost always too late to do this.

I speak, of course, about garages. Specifically, having enough open, clear, unclaimed, and uncluttered space in one that you can fit your car inside, along with the car of any hurricane guest, along with birdbaths, lawn flamingoes, and outdoor furniture.

I was pleased with myself last year when I reclaimed enough garage space to park my car inside and my parents's car as well—plus a birdbath—just as the storm started. I had only gotten started on the project after the last municipal trash pickup before the storm had come and gone. This meant that rather than throwing things out, I could only stack, box, and pack things into corners.

My final act of space reclamation was to position the front bumper of my car up against the pile of junk, boxes, and furniture that will undoubtedly be, within my lifetime, refinished and repaired, and then inch the vehicle slowly forward—rather in the manner of a bulldozer. I did this as the winds were picking up. I brought the garage door down and it cleared the car's rear bumper with a good half inch to spare.

Florida homes don't usually have basements. Crawl spaces in the roof are not convenient for long-term storage. This means the average Florida garage owner has a slightly different concept of what a garage is for than somebody from parts of the world where basements and attics are common. A garage is not a room made for a car. It's a storage room into which a car might be invited. Or not.

Now, with predictions of an active storm season in mind, I spent part of Memorial Day tackling the problem anew. This meant facing up to failed purchases and accepting that some once-wonderful technology is no longer of use to anyone. A realization that applies equally to popcorn makers and six hundred–baud external modems. This meant accepting that the lifetime of the average human allows one to refinish very few pieces of furniture. This meant accepting that some lamps are too ugly to fix.

And that's the problem with garage cleanup. It's not the physical effort; it's the pain of decision-making and the confronting of unpleasant realities.

On the upside, I did find a flashlight that had been lost since the Clinton administration. A powerful one, too. With a battery as big as a brick. Unfortunately, it had been a long time since the last emergency and, on inspection, the battery resembled a butterscotch-coated brick. The flashlight's insides were rust pudding. I'm sure it just needs a little cleanup. There was also an ugly lamp that still works and is only slightly chipped at the base, where you'd hardly notice.

Attack a garage right, in the calm before the storm, and you can be your own garage sale.

June 2005

After Charley—seeking close calls, revising the list

I awoke Saturday morning to the sound of chain saws. Two-stroke engines are not good to hear at any one-digit hour of the morning, but this was different. This was the sound of post-storm cleanup. It meant the dangers were past and everything from now on would involve familiar things. Things like saws, rakes, insurance forms, and public utilities.

I felt I was one of the fortunate because my roof was intact and the trees around my house were all standing, minus some impressive limbs. But you never feel truly lucky in a natural disaster merely for escaping major property damage; you must also have a close call. I do not know why luck is defined this way. One would think it would be great good luck simply to come out of a scary storm without anything to tell. One would think no storm at all would constitute the best luck of all. But no. Good luck does not live up to the name unless pushed a few notches in the direction of misfortune.

So I felt very fortunate to find an oak branch, six inches across at its ragged base, lying so close to my daughter's car the leaves touched the door and outer branches scratched the paint. A certified close call. Hugely lucky, despite other bumps the car endured. My daughter, however, felt very much otherwise.

I walked around the neighborhood in search of more close calls and quickly located massive oaks with their roots in the air. I saw limbs thick as fireplugs balanced on rooftops. Another ancient oak was folded in half, with the top leaning against a nearby roof. Lucky us.

At the height of the storm Friday night, the idea of needing to search for close calls would have seemed like a pretty good deal. In 70-plus-mph winds, an older wooden house makes sounds distressingly similar to a boat in bad weather. Outside, things were thumping and tearing in the blackness. Like a radio show, you had to imagine the action. People say hurricanes and tornadoes make a sound like a train, which is true enough. What people neglect to say is that they sound like a train that is going above your head. This is a major omission because it does rather add to the drama of the moment.

When I stepped out in the storm, just before the street lights went dark, the rain seemed to come from all directions at once—sideways, left and right, angling down, spraying up. Dark shapes whisked above my head, seemingly as big and fast and ugly as skyborne bikers. At that juncture, the lawn and tree damage I would later survey would have seemed a very acceptable outcome. So I have been trying to hold on to that moment. Even when the chain saws started. Even when the electricity didn't come back on the next day.

When you think of preparing for an electrical outage, you think of the obvious things—light and refrigeration. What I didn't foresee was coffee. This isn't just a cherished morning ritual, this is chemical dependency. I tried to shrug it off and drove to work on my bicycle—the better to navigate streets full of trees, tree parts, house debris, and lawn decorations. On my way, I saw a line of twenty-five people snaking out the door of Java Junction in Holly Hill.

Someone there had hooked a portable power generator to a coffee machine. Passing cars were slamming on their brakes, making U-turns and swerving across lanes of traffic to get to the coffee place's parking lot. I tried not to weep with gratitude. Thus fortified, I rode around downed trees and power lines and arrived in the newsroom very much like a functioning human being.

Tomorrow I'll think of something else. And next hurricane, I'll get a camp stove or something. Or a grill. I had turned down one street on the way back and was hit by the smell of charcoal and sausages grilling all mixed with fresh-cut green wood, chain-saw exhaust, gasoline, and pine needles. You can't bottle an aroma like that.

A grill: that's definitely on the new preparedness list. Right below batteries. And margarita mix. I had to crush the ice with a hammer when I got home, but one makes do in times of natural disaster.

August 2004

Hurricane Frances diary

Frances went on far longer than any hurricane needs to. This performance was over-the-top, excessive, and tasteless. What's worse, people who sat out two days and three nights of Frances someday will be the ones reminding anybody with the misfortune of sharing a shelter or home with them that the hurricane of the moment just doesn't measure up to the 2004 storm. The way people tiresomely rhapsodize about Hurricane Donna (1960).

"Frances wasn't one of these three-hours-of-thrashing-trees-and-everyone-goes-home storms," we'll say. "We're talking days of wood falling over your head and nights of the wind screaming outside your window. Two days, three days, four days . . . I forget how long. In those days we had real hurricanes."

But let's break this into days so we can all keep our stories straight:

Thursday. Preparation day

Because forecasters can track storms earlier and because Frances was a slow-moving storm, Floridians had more than two days to get ready. This was a good thing, but prodded people into overdoing it.

The psychology of panic-buying can be baffling. Sure, people created shortages of gas, plywood, and batteries. But why pudding? Shelves holding pudding in little plastic cups were picked clean. Evidently a lot of people thought the same thought: "Storm's a-brewin'—must have pudding."

Cookies, gone. Crackers, gone. Hot dog buns, gone. Atkins diets were this storm's first casualties.

Friday. Second preparation day

There is a little-studied effect of storm preparation I noted last week: Pre-Hurricane Driving Syndrome. It's an observable fact that the general level of driving skill drops off significantly immediately before a storm. Those afflicted by this syndrome lose the ability to swivel their heads when backing up and regard stop signs and traffic signals as intriguing possibilities rather than legal absolutes, particularly when transportation of plywood is involved. And because of the long lead-time and all-too-recent experiences with Hurricane Charley, many more windows were covered with plywood this time around.

I was, however, disappointed in the general lack of bull's-eyes, storm-swirls, and hurricane-related slogans spray painted on window plywood. Like "Hurricane Franny/Kiss my fanny," which was sprayed on one Holly Hill plywood window covering. Folks, these touches demonstrate a hearty mixture of defiance of the elements, fatalism, and an often-ribald sense of humor in time of crisis. We must do better next time. Compose your slogans in advance, write them down, and store them next to the batteries.

Saturday. Twenty-four hours of wind
I have learned to identify a half-dozen varieties of falling-wood noises. There's the single kettledrum thump of a big branch diving straight down. There's the shake, rattle, and roll of smaller branches hitting and rolling off the roof. The crack and ax-chop noises of medium branches breaking off and landing. All this is mixed with the many new and novel sounds a wooden house, a house whose sound-making you mistakenly thought you knew pretty well, can produce during a few days of sustained winds.

Sunday. Another twenty-four hours of wind
Before this weekend, I had never heard the phrase *feeder bands* used in a normal conversation. I do not care to hear it again. People compare hurricane winds to trains. I think they sound more like a roller coaster when you're standing in a ticket booth underneath. The coaster goes up and away and then louder and over your head. This is exciting for an hour. It is unpleasant after forty hours.

Monday. Crawling out
The rain hadn't stopped before the chain saws sputtered to life across town. People who had been shut in shelters and homes, often in the dark, were outside before the rain stopped. Even yard work is preferable to sitting in dark, hot rooms listening to radios and people talking about feeder bands amid ominous thudding outside.

Tuesday. Tracking a new storm
New definition of an optimist: somebody who takes down his plywood.

September 2004

Dr. Storms has your hurricane answers

Now that Florida has sustained four hurricanes in a row, the mental strain is starting to show in many folks. Even in the best of times, Floridians have a reputation for merrily inhabiting the orange zone of the ol' sanity meter, so these misfortunes have made things very bad indeed.

In the interest of better mental health, we have invited a noted self-help and hurricane-preparedness consultant to take your questions about coping effectively with the stresses of this hurricane season. So calm down, take the plywood off your windows, and Ask Dr. Storms:

Dear Dr. Storms—After the hurricanes, I feel the irresistible urge to strangle or throw things at anyone who uses the phrase hunker down. *I already had to buy a new television after putting a heavy flashlight through the screen, and I left fingerprints on the collar of a coworker. Am I oversensitive?*

Yours is an understandable and healthy reaction. It's common enough that there's even a name for it—*post-hurricane catch-phrase sensitivity.* Unfortunately, other professionals have a different name for it—*aggravated battery.* Yes, I, too, find that term judgmental and insensitive. But don't worry, no local jury would convict you. Plus, it's almost always pleaded down to time served.

Dear Dr. Storms—A coworker persists in asking me "Did you see the eleven o'clock five-day storm map?" and then laughs when I go running to the nearest television or computer. I'm afraid, though, that the one time I don't react, I'll find out too late there really is another hurricane bearing down on us.

I suggest you respond with this phrase: *Did you see your car?* Cultivate a knowing look of concern. Try it out in the mirror beforehand.

Dear Dr. Storms—My electricity only flickered a little in Hurricane Jeanne. Initially I was delighted, then I began feeling kind of bad because so many people didn't have power for days.

You are experiencing the classic symptoms of electricity guilt. You probably have avoided telling people about your good fortune and even kept the porch light off for fear of being the object of electrical envy. Like other forms of survivor's guilt, electricity guilt is best dealt with by remembering that storms are random things and you just lucked out this time. Given that luck is a finite resource, your good fortune makes it all the more likely that the next storm will take out your electricity and a three hundred-year-old oak tree will crush your carport like a Dixie Cup. Feel better now?

Dear Dr. Storms—It feels strange not to be tracking a storm. I feel listless and lonely now that I no longer have NOAA updates to listen to and follow.

This is a normal case of storm-tracking withdrawal. Perhaps you should track other disasters and prepare for them so that things feel normal. Perhaps a year-round phenomenon. I suggest volcanic eruptions.

Dear Dr. Storms—What kind of doctor are you, anyway? Does your field relate even remotely to hurricanes?

Dr. Storms's field is all about natural disasters. He has a PhD in holistic real estate and was adjunct professor in creative roofing at the Ocklawaha Institute of Home Repair, Stump Removal, and Professional Wrestling until its sad demise at the hands of small-minded regulators. He is a notary public and can perform weddings.

October 2004

Where were the hurricanes?
Dr. Storms answers critics

Dr. Storms broke into his emergency supply of bottled water, screwed off the top of the handiest bottle, plopped his feet up on his hurricane-supply box, and drank the contents in four gulps. It was hot outside, and he was disgusted.

Back in spring he had expected things would be cooking about now. That his phone would be ringing. That media types would be fighting among themselves to get statements from one of Florida's foremost unlicensed experts in hurricane-related mental health. That he'd be shouting against the wind while TV guys in rain slickers hung on his every word.

Instead it was a cloudless mid-August afternoon, and nobody seemed to know he was alive.

On the bright side, though, this means Dr. Storms has lots of spare time to answer your hurricane-related questions. So take this golden opportunity to Ask Dr. Storms:

Dear Dr. Storms—So what happened to that superactive, the-seas-will-churn-and-the-sun-will-be-blotted-from-the-sky hurricane season you predicted? Feeling a little dumb after telling everyone to do all this extreme preparedness stuff?

If you were really part of the culture of preparedness—a cool phrase of mine the governor picked up on—you wouldn't be asking a question like that. People who have never heard of the culture of preparedness will often prepare for things people expect. But it's preparing for things people don't expect and don't happen that mark a true preparedness expert.

Thus, buying flashlights during a hurricane sales-tax holiday is pretty lame preparedness. Having a lava barrier and wind gauge set in concrete in your backyard marks you as an arbiter of the culture of preparedness. So the fact that nothing I prepared for this year has actually happened only makes me feel better about myself.

Dear Dr. Storms—But it's August and there hasn't been one hurricane yet. Tropical storm names are only at "C." What happened to the ten-hurricane season you talked about on TV?

Dr. Storms is delighted somebody remembers his last television appearance. It seems so very long ago. But some summer day, his phone will ring again and sales of his books, *Managing the Inner Hurricane* and *150 Ways to Hunker Down*, will pick up again.

Nonetheless, he detects a note of peevishness in your query. Rest assured that Dr. Storms was only repeating what everybody else said. The National Weather Service predicted eight to ten storms. To sound authoritative, Dr. Storms merely eliminated the spread. People want certainty and ten is a good, round number.

Dear Dr. Storms—I should be happy at my good luck, and yet I feel oddly down and disappointed that nothing happened. What gives?

Near-hurricane letdown can lead to depression. Heavy television viewers are vulnerable since they spend days watching old footage of storms and swirling, color-enhanced radar maps that look like Grateful Dead T-shirts. This creates feelings of dread mixed with the thrill of possible adventure. Then it just stops and you resume your bland, meaningless life.

This can be particularly severe among people who have become used to being on TV and lauded for their expertise, but are now discarded, tossed aside by fickle television producers in a society that neither appreciates nor understands the culture of preparedness.

Dear Dr. Storms—How did the National Weather Service get away with revising its estimate halfway through the season? It seems like cheating. Does this affect the point spread in the office pool?

It does seem unfair. Especially since that estimate prompted Dr. Storms to print twice the number of business cards he would have otherwise. But no, this does not affect the hurricane office pool. It's like the horse races: nothing changes after the betting windows slam shut. See you in November, sucker.

Dear Dr. Storms—Weren't you sued or something?

In 2004 Dr. Storms playfully suggested the Hurricane Frances Drinking Game. This consisted of throwing back the libation of your choice each time a local or state official used the phrase *hunker down*. Little did he realize how popular that locution would become or how long the storm would last. This led to a rash of avoidable home accidents for which some litigious types imagined Dr. Storms had a contributing role. Silly, I know. But under terms of the settlements, he cannot say more.

Dear Dr. Storms—What kind of doctor are you, and how did you become a "hurricane-preparedness and emergency self-actualizing expert"?

Dr. Storms is a doctor of holistic real estate. He became a hurricane-preparedness and emergency self-actualizing expert while supervising a tree-removal crew after Hurricane Andrew. He figured there had to be an easier way to make a living. And, it turned out, there was.

August 2006

2 Somewhere on down the road

"Any driver who says he's lost lacks either imagination or salesmanship."

—*The Darwinian Gardener's Almanac*

Walter Boardman Lane, Ormond Beach. (Photo by Mark Lane)

State Road A1A, Beverly Beach

How do you save funky beachside areas during a condo boom? And who would want to try? These are questions being asked the length of A1A. And they feel more urgent now that I read about another campground/ recreational-vehicle park/mobile- and sort-of-mobile-home place (with bait shop) being sold to a condo developer. Units will sell between $600,000 and $950,000. And this is in Beverly Beach, in northeast Flagler County. An area that hitherto has been nicely resistant to change.

We have environmental preservation zones. We have historic sites. But who's looking out for the low-rent beachside? The weathered beachside bar with concrete tables outside? The oddly placed private campground? The trailer parks that make no economic sense? The mom-and-pop motel with hand-painted signs that were constructed as sure things in the days before the interstate highway system? Barbecue places (that also sell bait) with a service counter facing the road and the sea oats?

Nope, nobody. There is no official state Funky Beach Area designation. No LD/FBT-1 (Low Density/Funky Beach Town—Level 1) zoning on a county master plan map.

If you didn't live there, you're not likely to miss the Singing Surf Campground or Picnicker's Campground, the place farther up A1A in Painters Hill that had earlier this year been sold for condos, too. Manufactured housing with an ocean view defies economic gravity. And it's not all that scenic from the road, either.

And yet, hasn't this always been part of the great rural Florida dream? You know, the dented Airstream trailer parked in sight of the dunes by a guy who chucked it all in Jersey sometime after the furnace failed and the rumors started about the plant closing. He parked there because the rain got too bad to keep driving south, then the sun came out, and it looked good—and that was five years ago. You don't hear that kind of story that much anymore.

And you're going to hear it even less. The gaps in the condo curtain between A1A and the ocean fill in a little more every year. You see either protected natural land or high-end investment property and little in between.

We might be able to protect a few stretches of dune here and there and get a walkway between the buildings, but the kind of everyman's beach site that used to be taken as a Florida birthright is fast disappearing. And low-slung, beach-town places are harder to find with each passing year.

Last spring, as I bicycled around Anna Maria Island, on the gulf side of the state, I was delighted at having discovered the place in time. They have a twenty-seven-foot building-height cap there, bless them. (Down from the previous thirty-seven-foot cap.) No chain hotels or fast-food insta-buildings. I ordered beer and a grouper sandwich from a waitress in cutoffs at a place that was hanging off a short pier at a noticeable tilt and leaned back in a plastic lawn chair to enjoy the sunset.

This was like the Keys, say, twenty years ago. Or at least the way I choose to remember them twenty years ago. A place that didn't try to look like a golf course. A place where the ocean was not walled off. Who knows how long this will last? Or when I'll find myself traveling to places that remind me of Flagler Beach?

Anymore, places in Florida choose between anonymous sprawl or gated, fussy gentrification. The funky beachside place with roads of broken shell and small, weathered-wood beach houses that need paint is an alternative that just makes no economic sense. Like a campground/RV park by the sea.

October 2005

U.S. Highway 1, Holly Hill

Let us pause to mourn the passing of Mr. Peanut. The towering fifty-four-foot sign stood by the side of U.S. 1 in Holly Hill, near Daytona Beach, for almost forty years, pointing to a squat little center of commercial enterprise called Points East Plaza.

He wasn't Mr. Peanut when he was carted away. Every U.S. 1 commuter knows that. He was Mr. Tuxedo-Dude With a Bad Haircut. But for most his career as a U.S. 1 eyesore—1958–1970—he was Mr. Peanut, the natty, top-hatted legume and registered trademark of Planters peanut products.

It was a drive-by landmark of my childhood. Holly Hill's totem. There's something about a four-story sheet-metal depiction of a monocled peanut that grabs a motorist's attention. One arm akimbo, the other gesturing with a sleek, black cane, it overcame U.S. 1's nearby visual competition with patrician ease.

But, alas, U.S. 1 became a different thoroughfare up and down America between 1958 and 1970. With Interstate 95 complete, the carloads of tourists cruising in search of peanuts stopped coming. I try to picture the customers in those distant days, driving their Ford Falcons, scanning the Florida roadway in search of peanuts. "Where can a guy find a decent peanut log in this burg?" they'd sputter in exasperation to nobody in particular. And then, they'd see him beckoning, a towering Mr. Peanut. Their vacation was saved.

The peanut shop was sold and converted to a grocery. The sign was sold and converted to a grocer. A peanut-shaped grocer with an oddly shaped head, but nonetheless a recognizable grocer with a white apron. It was a creative coup for Wiggins's Grocery. The landmark stood.

Eight years later, the business changed again. Holly Hill held its breath. The transformation of a foppish peanut to peanut-shaped grocer by now had rooted itself in the popular imagination. What would Art Mart do with the sign?

The store's owners responded to this challenge with artistic creativity. They, too, kept the sign. It was repainted to depict a peanut-shaped artist with goatee and black beret pointing a brush at the new art store. Certainly more bohemian than the elegant goober or the stolid grocer, but U.S. 1 was not a judgmental place by the 1970s and had seen its share of arty-looking types. The beatnik stayed.

By 1978, however, the site was occupied by a tile company and real estate and insurance offices, none of which wished to be represented by a beatnik. The owners hit upon Mr. Tuxedo-Dude With a Bad Haircut. It was, I guess, supposed to suggest the elegance of the address. But it is often difficult to get elegance across when your medium is a badly corroded, fifty-four-foot sheet-metal sign.

I respected the owners's attempt to comply with local custom and adapt to the Mr. Peanut motif. Unfortunately, Mr. Tuxedo-Dude With a Bad Haircut just didn't cut it.

The site now houses Alpha Therapeutic Plasma Center. Someone suggested complying with tradition and repainting Tuxedo-Dude With a Bad Haircut into a peanut-shaped doctor gesturing with a giant hypodermic needle. This was rejected. I do not know why. So another landmark comes down.

I have gauged my progress on U.S. 1 by Mr. Peanut from the time I was a small child. Now it's gone, and the side of road looks even more like U.S. 1 just about anywhere else: cookie-cutter strip malls, prefab burger dispensaries, gas stations, and orphaned mom-and-pop motels.

Ugly commercial signage is not high on anyone's historic preservation list. Yet once in a while it does a lot of the things distinctive old architecture does. It marks a familiar place. It is our local inside joke. It becomes a connection with our past.

After a few decades on the job, Mr. Peanut no longer pointed to a business; it pointed the way home.

March 1997

Interstate 4, Celebration exit

On Thanksgiving, the nation divides itself into hosts and travelers. The latter are the majority. We fill the airports. We take to the roads. I have always been a Thanksgiving traveler. After my sister moved across the state, I moved from being a cross-town Thanksgiving traveler to a cross-state traveler.

I used to get upset when I'd head west and hit the parking lot that is the Celebration exit, west of Orlando. But now, as I slow to stop, I feel I'm participating in a kind of holiday tradition. I'm in the car parade of Thanksgiving guests.

People from around the state parked fender by fender next to fly-in diners from other places who are puzzling out the controls on their rental cars and rolling down their windows to feel the warm air. Not like back home.

I turn off the motor and put on holiday music (*The Allman Brothers Band at Fillmore East*) and roll down the windows. I imagine the overturned tanker ahead is spilling cranberry sauce. And around me, I watch my fellow Thanksgiving travelers talking into cell phones. I know what they're saying.

I know we said we'd be there by now, but we're stuck on the road. You can warm it in the microwave . . .

I know what the custody agreement said, but it's not noon yet. Last year, the deputy distinctly said not to call them before 3 p.m. . . .

I know you gave me a map with the Apopka route on it. This just seemed simpler. We're sure to be there by dessert. Yeah, dessert this year . . .

I think it's only a basic health precaution to cook it another forty-five minutes, and that would put everything at just the right time. Anything less would be irresponsible and leave you open to real civil liability. No, I'm not joking . . .

Thanksgiving is one of our more do-it-yourself holidays. You are freer to design and maintain your own traditions. And the parking lot outside Orlando is mine. When I glide to a stop outside Celebration, it feels like the holiday has started. I can smell the stuffing.

I look at the road around me with a critic's eye. Some orange traffic barrier drums have been rearranged since last November. Some mountains of dirt seem to have migrated. I could swear there is earth-moving machinery parked exactly where I remember them from last year. And that's another part of my Thanksgiving: giving thanks that the sprawl and gridlock radiating from Orlando hasn't quite made it to my coast.

Some tell me this holiday tradition, like so many others, may pass. That in the next decade I-4 will be widened and there will be no orange traffic drums. That a toll lane would help. That hydrogen-powered cars with antigravity drive will break up the bottleneck.

But the Celebration exit jam is a constant and will remain so until global warming makes this a beach-ramp traffic backup. It is a standing feature of I-4. Like a river or spring. It should appear on road maps, show up on satellite photos, and be part of anyone's repertoire of travelers' directions. ("Just past the giant hotel that looks like a spaceship . . . keep going until you reach the traffic pileup.")

My kids taunt me about how I can still sound surprised every time we hit it and must utter a ritual curse upon Florida's sprawl-friendly, build-anywhere land policies. I bore them with talk of road-building concurrency goals.

Well-meaning relatives offer involved alternative routes that involve advanced orienteering skills and a grasp of GPS technology. I'll have none of it.

There are holiday traditions to uphold.

November 2005

U.S. Highway 1, Ormond Beach city limits

Hard to believe it's been more than half a year since Hurricane Summer. Sometimes I'll be driving somewhere, and I'll still find myself noticing some new aftereffect of the storms. Like the Billboard That Isn't There.

Like most people, I'm better at noticing things that are there as opposed to things that are not. The human mind just works that way. I notice blue tarps every time I go outside. But it's only on reflection that I think, hey, wasn't there a big oak tree over there? Didn't that yard used to have a fence? Didn't that house used to have a roof?

Because it isn't there, it took me months to notice the Billboard That Isn't There. When I did notice it, I felt surprised and happy but a little dumb.

There was a time before last summer when the Billboard That Isn't There was the Billboard That Is There. Or, more precisely, the Billboard at the Edge of the Marsh. One of a set of three or four.

I hated the Billboard at the Edge of the Marsh. Usually when there's something ugly along your habitual routes, you get used to it. Any habitual U.S. 1 driver has a very high tolerance for ugly. We even have some affection for things that are ugly in a homey, evocative, or creative way. I rather pride myself on being able to pick out and notice vintage ugly U.S. 1 signage from among the bland, new, and ugly plastic stuff.

But the Billboard at the Edge of the Marsh (now known as the Billboard That Isn't There) and its neighbors were different. The marsh, canals, and grassland they obscured make for a refreshing scenic break in a generally unlovely drive. The marsh and water are fringed with trees in the distance, and you can see just a few nicks of the railroad track on the horizon.

This is all at the edge of town. An area that for a U.S. 1 driver is the town's back door. When I reach the spot, I tell myself I'm almost home. An evocative stretch of Florida road right before the edge-of-town kind of buildings pick up again.

But there, stuck in the middle of this landscape, was this big old sign. Like a price tag on a painting. *Sale! Marked down drastically!*

Rather than becoming invisible over time, this felt more annoying with time. I tried to mentally erase it.

Have you ever noticed that when you try not to notice something, your eyes will always be drawn toward that very thing? Well, that's how it worked.

I hated that billboard for years and heartily wished for a strong wind to blow it away. Then, strange to say, a strong wind came and blew it away. Most of it, anyway.

Still, this didn't register right away. The one good thing to come out of the hurricane for me, and it took months for me to be aware that I was enjoying the view and not looking at the Billboard That Isn't There and the signs next to it.

The remains are not things of beauty, either. Their wooden skeletons lean at odd angles, though are still standing in a tentative and uncertain manner. Stripped of their commercial messages and twisted into interesting shapes, they seem to work with the landscape and even blend in, in a forlorn, U.S. 1 kind of way.

It will be a while before we know how much highway beautification Hurricane Summer brought to Florida. Sign companies are suing to rebuild wherever they can, and cities and counties are so far doing a generally good job of resisting.

Naturally I'm rooting for the weather to finish the work on this stretch of road. I'll be more careful to notice after the next big wind.

March 2005

Postscript: The Billboard That Isn't There still isn't there.

State Road A1A, St. Augustine

Once again I found myself leaning on the railing of the alligator pit. I do this every so often. Watching the alligator pit gets me in touch with my roots. My roots as somebody who grew up in a tourist town. My roots as a Floridian. My roots as a political writer.

There are few alligator farms left in Florida. Only fourteen were counted as active by the Fish and Wildlife Conservation Commission in 2004, and most were not tourist-attraction kind of places.

The Florida alligator farm has gone the way of the jungle cruises, the fabled all-you-can-drink orange juice stands ("two cups *is* all you can drink,") parrot shows, tropical gardens, and other lost-era tourist attractions.

I am not discriminating in my appreciation for the last alligator farms. Personally I go for volume. Quantity not quality. I'm not into the shows. I do not want multimedia. I deduct points for outdoor speakers and video screens.

I want the traditional Florida alligator farm, which is a pit and lots of carnivorous reptiles. Anything else is an extra that is out of the spirit of things.

And the St. Augustine Alligator Farm has always been my alligator farm of choice, even when it still had competition. The St. Augustine farm stuck to the basics: lots of pit, lots of alligators supplemented by a handful of things with fangs, and a few star reptiles.

When I went back there—on a weekday, no less—the place was bustling with kids from summer camp (identified by matching yellow T-shirts and sharing my purist's enthusiasm for the pit), as well as tourists carrying impressive digital cameras and speaking the languages of Germany, Brazil, Latin America, and New Jersey. Compare that to the woebegone state of Marineland, less than twenty miles down State Road A1A, and its longevity is even more remarkable.

Somehow, since 1893, the St. Augustine Alligator Farm has always managed to morph into the alligator farm the times demanded. The St. Augustine Alligator Farm of my childhood was pleasantly cheesy. Big pits, lots of U.S. 1 billboards, corny promotions, the gator sliding board, and in the gift store, View-Master disks that showed jaws popping out at you. Now it's the St. Augustine Alligator Farm Zoological Park. More natural. Bigger on Wonders-of-the-Planet-We-All-Share stuff. No alligator-wrestling or jungle noises pumped through scratchy speakers.

But it has not abandoned its roadside attraction roots. It still has Gomek. Gomek used to be the place's star attraction. A seventeen-foot, seventeen-hundred-pound crocodile from New Guinea, it was huge, impressive, and, as park personnel testify in a video commentary playing in the Gomek Room, a reliable showbiz pro during the raw-meat-feeding-time shows.

And who was something of a personification of Florida Values: he came here from far away, seemed to take life as it came along, didn't move much in the summer, and was okay with the tourists.

Gomek's death of heart failure in 1997 at close to eighty years old would have been a blow to a less resourceful institution. Instead, they stuffed the guy in a suitably fearsome neck-stretched-for-feeding-time pose and he became an even bigger draw. And less maintenance.

In the gift store, "Gomek Forever" T-shirts and mugs outnumber those of Maximo, his living successor. A pro even in death. I suspect that as a stuffed attraction, he's going to outlast Lenin.

July 2006

State Road A1A, Flagler Beach

Every time I drive State Road A1A where it hugs the coast through Flagler County and the northern tip of Volusia, I silently bless the road engineers. Even last week, as a few chunks of the road south of Flagler Beach were threatening to fall into the ocean. Again.

Thank you, oh, road engineers long gone, for placing this road in so precarious a spot. For if A1A had been built only a little farther west—say a hundred and fifty feet or so—this would be a very different place. No long drives with an undulating view of sea oats and palmetto. No weathered decks, wooden stairways down to the beach, and beach cruisers leaning against speed-limit signs.

Instead, it would likely be a mix of motels, condos, and parking lots. High rise condos and pink hotels require a certain amount of space— although not as much as you think. And the placement of A1A didn't leave much space between road and sea through southern Flagler County and northern Volusia County. The result is that you can get a pre-condo view of the dunes from out of your car windows. On one side of the car, anyway.

And all because the people in 1927 who hammered stakes in the ground marking the path of Oceanshore Boulevard as a beachside road made the not-unreasonable assumption that the shoreline would pretty much stay put. If only they'd kept doing that farther south.

Although the road's placement has been an excellent barrier to bad coastal development, there is this downside. Parts of the road are falling into the ocean.

Hurricanes threatened to undermine the road last year and tropical storms continued the work this year.

To save the road, the state department of transportation has dropped coquina boulders, granite, and sand on some dunes east of the road near Flagler Beach. At intervals the mix is covered with a heavy dark vinyl. This saves the road but ruins the beach.

You can't walk barefoot on jagged granite, and the chunks have rolled into areas nearby where people can still surf and swim. Sandpipers can't run on rocks. And rock-armored dunes can worsen beach erosion overall, over time. With time, and not even very much time, rocks sink into the sand and do not do much good there. They are, everyone recognizes, a seasonal fix only.

The state has been talking about building sea walls that would save the road but obliterate the beach. Renowned beach geologist Orrin Pilkey calls the process of building and rebuilding sea walls next to a disappearing beach *New Jerseyization*.

A chilling term, that. There is no easy or cheap solution here. You move the road inland at immense expense and inevitable public opposition. You commit to full New Jerseyization immense expense and inevitable public opposition. You dump new sand on the beach at immense expense and watch it wash into the sea. Or figure out something new and amazing that may or may not work. All pretty unpalatable.

Just don't blame the people who put the road stakes down in the '20s. The land they built on had stayed in the same place for as long as anybody had known about. Who could have predicted that as soon as the road was built, sea levels around the planet would steadily begin rising?

This started around the 1930s, depending on which study you use. The sea-level rise averages about three millimeters a year. In North Florida, the sea level, as measured by the National Oceanic and Atmospheric Administration, has risen at a rate of 2.43 millimeters a year, or 7.5 inches since A1A was built.

So bless you and curse you, Flagler road-builders. You were caught in the forces of long-term storm-cycles, geological shifts, global warming, and sea-level rise and left us with the bill. At least you saved the view. And on days like this, that seems worth it.

October 2005

Old Dixie Highway, unincorporated Volusia County

The shiny blue pickup truck filled my rearview mirror end to end and up and down. The driver was, evidently, a man in a hurry and felt he might communicate his sense of urgency by keeping an unvarying eight inches between his front bumper and my rear bumper. Unfortunately, he was driving in a no-hurry zone of a no-hurry road on a no-hurry day of the week. It was a beautiful Sunday afternoon on the stretch of road known locally as the Loop.

Keeping the eight-inch space took so much concentration that he had to put down his cell phone and grip the wheel with both hands. I suppose he was singing along with the radio because his mouth was moving even though nobody else was in the cab.

The Loop is a twenty-three-mile belt of road that winds through marsh and oak forests and shows off what a lovely place we live in. This is not a commuter road—not yet, anyway. If you are here, you are here to gawk, enjoy the tunnel of tree limbs, or point at birds. This is not a point-A-to-point-B drive.

The road straightened and the truck shot past me. I chuckled inwardly. Within a half mile, he would find himself behind a small group of bicyclists and then a large group of motorcyclists. Everyone in front of him was united by a shared determination not to be in a hurry going through a forest on a Sunday. Whether he planned on it or not, he was taking the scenic route.

The tranquility of the Loop is increasingly marred by new development and heavier traffic. I suppose, given the history of Florida sprawl, this is inevitable. But countermeasures might be possible.

As the blue pickup barreled around the next turn, it occurred to me that by poking along the road, I was sending a message about the kind of road I took Old Dixie Highway to be. This is nobody's shortcut or freeway. It's a road to savor. And those who want to live out in the woods had better like looking at the woods, because they'll be spending a lot of time doing just that all the way into town. At least if they're behind me.

Now, what if everyone who thought that way drove that way? It wouldn't even be civil disobedience. There's no sign saying you *can't* drive slowly. And if everyone did it, nobody with a job could live out that way.

It would take hours to do the smallest errand. The Loop would be saved without the government doing anything.

Clearly I was on to something. If enough people formed a perpetual slow-motion roadblock on roads like this, there would be much less pressure to develop wild areas into houses and golf courses.

I emerged from the scenic drive and stepped on the gas to turn onto State Road A1A where I found traffic backed up behind somebody going 28 mph, oblivious to a line of fourteen cars following closely. It appeared that somebody else already was on to this tactic.

Florida has long been known for slow-motion drivers. People have always attributed it to the large proportion of older drivers and tourists with only a vague idea of where they are. But do we really know this for sure?

Maybe this is a political statement. No, a movement. A stand against overdevelopment, but nobody got around to letting me know.

I had lots of time to think about this all the way home.

August 2003

North Ridgewood Avenue, Ormond Beach

Florida bicycle riders lead lives of excitement and danger. It's part of what makes our existence so glamorous. Like the other day when I was intentionally run off the road for the second time in as many weeks.

This was not a big deal because I was riding a mountain bike, and driving in the dirt is, well, what the thing is designed to do. And as a newspaper columnist, I'm no stranger to inspiring random hostility from people I've never met. Still, I'm always disconcerted when people try to kill me without knowing where I work. I'm sensitive that way.

I was riding along a 25-mph residential street when a white car, which would have been described as a luxury sedan two owners ago, pulled next to me. The driver was in his 20s, with shoulder-length hair, and looked like he might be a roadie for an Aerosmith tribute band. Fans of '80s-era heavy-metal don't fit the usual profile of a cyclist hassler. These tend to be older, heavier, and more upscale.

"You're supposed to be on the sidewalk," he shouted.

An amazing number of people drive under the misapprehension that bicyclists ride the roads in flagrant violation of law, custom, and morality. In fact, nearly all city ordinances in the state allow bikers the choice of road or sidewalk, except for where they are banned from sidewalks. State law allows bikes on all roads except limited-access roads. And if you have the wind at your back and are tooling along in high gear at 20 mph, an uneven sidewalk littered with storm debris awaiting removal is a bad idea, even if drivers at intersections regularly took any notice of what's coming down the sidewalk, which they don't.

I told the guy he was wrong and kept pedaling. At such moments, I can never remember the right statute numbers. (They are Florida Statutes 316.2065(1), 316.2065(5)(a) and 316.091(4) for next time.)

"You're a (pithy Anglo-Saxon-derived expletive) moron and you're getting off the road," Metal Dude told me. He drove even with me and pulled to the side until his two right tires were kicking up dirt and grass. He drove that way for about half a block.

Presented for your consideration: here's a guy who is driving with two tires off the road and one hand on the wheel. He is looking out his passenger window and screaming. Why? To deliver a lecture on traffic safety. And why is this guy who is driving at bicyclist speed with two wheels off the road so eye-poppingly, mouth-droolingly, vein-bulgingly furious? Because I'm making him late.

"I hope you fall off your little bike, get run over, and die!" he shouted, by way of farewell.

And I hope you never change, metal-dude.

This would not be worth recalling if it were an isolated, and perhaps drug-assisted, case of metal-head road rage. But it's not. It's what a frequent cyclist expects. Different only in degree and vividness of expression.

The driver who had run me off the road the week before was an older guy who pretty thoroughly filled the bucket seat of his SUV. I suspect he meant only to get close enough to scare me but didn't have quite enough control of the car. He would have needed to push the power-window button to get verbally confrontational, so that part wasn't worth the exertion.

This was on a scenic road that attracts motorcyclists and bicyclists from all over. But it's increasingly used by cars driven by busy people who don't care about the view. As a result, anyone on two wheels can count on having someone yelling, leaning on the horn for a half mile, or swerving in close to make a point.

I don't know why so many normal people turn into distracted, hyperventilating, homicidal mouth-breathers the moment they settle into a car. I have a theory that it's in part because we treat the windshield as though it's a wide-screen TV, and nothing around our plastic and metal cocoon seems terribly real. But maybe it has to do with the frustrations of commuting longer distances on roads that are ever more overcrowded and torn up. More bad social fallout from sprawl. Don't know.

What I have discovered is that the mere sight of bicyclists sometimes triggers instant road rage. Even on low-speed residential streets. It just does. Mimes are more popular than bicycle riders.

Still, I refuse to be chased off the road. Just don't blame me if you see me riding across your front lawn. I'm getting pretty good at evasive maneuvers.

October 2004

U.S. Highway 92, Daytona Beach

There are two seasons on the road—elbow-out-the-window season and elbow-inside season.

These seasons are supposed to take turns. Elbows protected by glass against winds of winter. Elbows emerging like groundhogs to sense spring. Elbows recoiling from the sun as the air conditioner kicks on for summer. Elbows emerging for the breezes of fall.

This is, right now, window-down season. The best moments of it. I thought everyone knew this. Yet I look out at stalled traffic and am dismayed at the lack of public awareness of what should be the natural order of the streets. Almost everything on the road has its windows up tight.

My children are confused by this. Kids in their early teens are very alert for signs that their families are not normal. I must try to explain that it is, indeed, normal and even preferable for car windows to be open part of the year.

"This is Florida," I say. "If you are old enough to drive a car, your left arm is supposed to be darker or redder than your right. It is the privilege of residency. The badge of the native. The sign of a commuter with an appreciation for nature and the rhythm of seasons."

They are dubious and whine for air that has been conditioned and conditioned a lot. They are wrong. It is not yet time.

In front of us, a line of more than a dozen cars is stopped waiting for a train the length of New Jersey to roll past. I take this as an opportunity for closer social research. Yes, the kids are correct. We are in the minority for having our windows down. I look up and down the line for signs of human elbows.

The first one is only two cars ahead, jutting from a convertible with its top folded down. The kind of car that's become a symbol of midlife reassessment, a convertible in a hue that might be described as Rogaine-red. The driver, one may assume, has a developed sense of his mortality. One that drives him to do more than drive with an elbow in the wind. He wants to be in the wind his whole self. He wants to be all elbow. I applaud him.

The other two arms are from pickup trucks. One of them has a pleasing driver-passenger symmetry—elbow on one side, dog's nose on the other.

All the remaining cars by the rail crossing are shut tight as jam jars, idling in place. They don't understand what's at stake.

I regard the button marked *A/C* with wariness. (And why is it *A/C* and not *A.C.* or *AC*? Another mystery of industrial design.) If I were to touch that button out of a misguided sense of social conformity and exaggerated respect for automobile aerodynamics, spring would grind to a halt, replaced by relentless summer.

This has happened before. I've seen it, done it, and take full responsibility (but no blame or legal liability). Hit that button and we will be sealed in cars and buildings for months, consoled only by the hum of compressors. I must hold out for the sake of spring.

The kids see this as eccentricity. They think climate-control is their friend, their year-round friend. They think I'm a cheapskate, a stupid-head, and a tyrant out of touch with popular opinion. They lay out their case: "It's just an air conditioner. The wind messes up my hair. We're going to sweat and die."

But I'm helping them by slowing time. If spring zips by a car window without blowing against you, you might miss it. Our machines hold the elements at bay, but in the process let us forget where we are in a year.

An open window is better than a calendar. Trust a person with a tan elbow to know where he is.

Now, everyone shut up back there.

May 1998

Interstate 10, Baker County

In Florida, there is no fast lane. This frustrates people who come from states where, by law and custom, fast drivers use the left lane and slower drivers and speed-limit abiders use the right. In Florida we drive in whichever lane has the nicest view, works best with radio reception, or sends a message to the cars immediately behind us.

I have found this philosophy off the road as well. You arrive at the airports of most major non-southern American cities or anywhere in the Commonwealth of Nations and you will notice slower-moving or non-moving people standing on the right side of escalators, moving sidewalks, and hallways, leaving the left for people on the run. You land in Florida and everybody plops themselves in the middle or on the left or wherever.

It's our way of letting people know, as soon as they get off the plane, that Florida is not about efficiency or getting someplace. This is the Sunshine State. It is not the Getting Somewhere State.

Some are frustrated by these lax practices and folkways. Particularly on the highway.

And while legislative enactments are blunt instruments for changing people's habits, some see no choice. Thus, a law aimed at slowpokes in the left lane was taken up by the Florida Senate's Transportation Committee last week. The vote deadlocked 4–4. This won't kill the bill outright, but like two logging trucks going side by side at 45 mph for the length of two counties along I-10, it does make reaching the station on time unlikely.

This is the third year in a row some kind of legislation addressing this problem has been before the legislature. In 2005 this was called the Road Rage Reduction Act and was passed by the legislature only to be vetoed by then-governor Jeb Bush.

Bush complained there was no research showing the bill had anything at all to do with the problem it claimed to be solving. Which was true enough, but what if we demanded that of *everything* the legislature did? It would be the end of politics as we know it.

The big objection to the bill is that if you're in the left lane because you see slow traffic ahead and to the right, or a road obstruction, or know that you soon need to turn left, and there's an aggressive driver behind you who has his heart set on breaking the sound barrier somewhere up the road, you could be the one charged with careless driving. It would punish small-time speeders for failing to make way for big-time speeders.

This issue keeps coming up before the legislature because, by accident of history and demographics, our state capital is in the most inconvenient spot possible without actually being on an island with electric fencing and sharks in the harbor.

This means that legislative staff, lobbyists, advisors, lawyers, press, and those legislators who don't find private plane rides get to spend a lot of time contemplating the pine barrens along I-10 and watching traffic pile up behind a rolling roadblock of poky cars, vans with two-by-fours for bumpers, and trucks that take three counties to reach their upper gears.

This issue may be dead for now, but it's only one traffic jam away from a new and quite thorough firsthand re-examination. There's nothing like spending a half hour in The Greater Olustee Area to inspire strong opinions on reforming the state's traffic habits.

This trip across the state, I decided conclusively, somewhere near the Baker County line, that this debate is far from over.

February 2007

State Road 40, Ormond Beach

A close brush with death can change everything. The sky is bluer. The air more fragrant. The coffee richer. That last item, the coffee, was the very thing that almost led to my demise.

I was on my way to my favorite coffee place, but I got distracted. Another sorry case of roadway zone-out. The sort of thing that happens when you get in a car and automatically drive home or to work, forgetting anything else on your itinerary. I drove past the coffee place.

As a direct result, I was dazedly barreling down the boulevard at just the moment a Buick swerved off the road, knocked over a streetlight, and skidded through the front window of the café. Wood splintered and the window exploded, glass sprayed everywhere.

Nobody was seriously hurt, but I would have changed that. Had I been there sipping a latte, I would have turned around upon hearing the brakes squeal and spilled my drink. I'd have bent over to wipe it up and that would be the last thing I'd have seen in this mortal coil. A pool of latte—with cocoa, not cinnamon.

And who knows what might have happened to the co-owner, Brad? As it was, just before this happened, he was outside sitting in a green plastic chair and saw four customers headed toward the front door. He got up to help pour coffee, and boom! in came the car. It crushed the green chair like a bug while he was safely behind the counter.

And the four customers? They might have thought about hanging out by the front door, in the path of imminent danger. But instead they saw Brad bustling behind the counter, and, drawn by the smell of fresh coffee, they walked right in, bellied up to the bar, then boom! the car came through the window. Brad saved their lives by doing what coffee-guys are supposed to do, keeping the java flowing. He's a credit to the industry.

And Mike, the owner? He considered sitting in the chair on the sidewalk, too, but instead he went in and handled this influx of business. Then crash! the Buick came through the window.

Those four mysterious customers, therefore, saved the lives of Mike and Brad by drawing them safely inside and behind the counter. They changed the course of history.

And me? I'm glad somebody asked. If I had had better powers of concentration, I would have followed my original itinerary, walked into the place and been standing around figuring out whether I would order a large latte or small latte. (Large latte or small latte? Large latte or small latte?)

Mike would have given up on me and walked outside. The four customers would have looked in the window, decided I was a difficult customer, and paused by the front window.

The result: We all would have been in the path of the car. I would have spilled my drink, and everyone else would have been distracted by my apologies and would not be looking for any traffic that might come through the window. Close call.

But National Public Radio should not be forgotten. If I had not been listening to *All Things Considered*, my mind would not have wandered quite so far. And I would have remembered to stop for coffee. And then history, mine anyway, would have been altered. This means all those people who called in during pledge week were actually saving human lives.

I know, you're probably asking yourself at this point how El Nino–influenced weather patterns affected this chain of events. Good question. El Nino saved my life. It caused an unusually warm, rainy spring in Florida. This meant I was in even more of a daze because it was an unusually warm, humid spring day, and I was listening to the car radio, with the car windows open, humming to myself. This meant I missed my turn.

Yup, we don't know how lucky we are. We walk through our daily lives streaming a roll of causality behind us in time like toilet paper stuck to our soles.

One little thing changes and the whole picture alters. I may have saved you from tragedy just by writing this. And I wouldn't have written this had I stopped for coffee. So you, too, gentle reader, are part of the chain. You had a very close call. Smell the coffee.

April 1998

U.S. Highway 1, Boulogne

I'm standing on a weathered concrete bridge, facing west in a slow drizzle. An undertaking that seems dubious because whenever a lumber truck rattles across, the structure shakes more than seems entirely reasonable.

Below me is the St. Marys River, its banks covered in vines which in the rain seem to be glowing green and lengthening as I look at them. As best I can tell, my left foot is in Florida and my right foot is in Georgia.

Tourists do this, you know. Something compels them everywhere in the world to stand with one foot on painted lines and brass survey markers worn smooth by this repeated exercise. At the southern end of this road they dutifully lean against the U.S. 1 "end" sign in Key West for photographs. (And why is it the end and not the beginning? Tell me that.) Out west, they find places where three or four big square states come together and must, absolutely must, stand there. As though that point taps into the intersecting energies of four distinctly different fields.

Well, the energies of Georgia and North Florida never felt that different. Some might characterize them as a distinct lack of energy. Particularly in the summer.

This point used to be Florida's front door. The first sight of the Sunshine State for car-driving travelers. First when this was Dixie Highway, and then when it was U.S. 1.

So if you arrived in Florida between the 1920s and the 1960s, there's a good chance this was the exact spot you entered the state. Interstate 95 would not be completed to the state line until 1971. So in standing here, I was going through an exercise of retracing my steps. Anything that went wrong happened somewhere down the road that way.

There's still a blue sign here that says "FLORIDA" just past the bridge. Nothing elaborate. It was put up as part of a minipark in 1965 ("In memory of Josephine Bay Paul. Philanthropist and lover of beauty . . .") and looks like the entrance to a subdivision that was a nice place thirty years ago.

Beyond it, a little over a mile south, near Hilliard, are the ruins of the Florida welcome station. The welcome station was among the first in the nation when it was built in 1951. It is the backdrop of my first identifiable Florida memory, something I have in common with a lot of people my age.

At age seven I was not a good sport about traveling. I was a whiner, was too nearsighted to play the count-the-cows car games, and would throw up out the station-wagon window at unpredictable intervals.

We stopped at the welcome station, drank free orange juice in the shade, and studied maps and glossy brochures. A relief from the boredom of rural driving.

I threw up near Callahan.

The welcome station has been out of use for twenty years. Ferns grow inside. It's been boarded up so long the plywood is weathered and warped. You can make out an outline of Florida drawn in mold where the sign used to be. The concrete picnic tables where I drank orange juice are still there, though.

The welcome station is emblematic of much of this route. You see the ruins with a sign that says "Truc Stop" that used to be a major truckers' depot, the sprawling beige assisted-living center that used to be a sprawling pink motel, the other motel that is a motorcycle repair shop, and the motel office that has been painted turquoise and turned into a cramped bar. There's a hand-lettered sign without vowels advertising "BL's BBQ," and the Hi-Lite Motel sign makes no claim more grand than that its rooms are "tidy."

I often scan my way on U.S. 1 with the eye of an archaeologist, picking up hints of what was here in a distant pre-Disney, pre-interstate roadside world. U.S. 1 was the primary connector of Florida's east coast from 1929 until about 1970. In the typical Florida east coast town, if you want to measure the distance between what was there before the 1920s land boom and what came after, draw a line between U.S. 1 and the center of downtown. If you want to measure the next half century of sprawl, measure the distance between U.S. 1 and the interstate.

This means that driving any random part of U.S. 1 is to find evidence of the buildings, economy, and landscape of a few generations ago. It cuts through towns like a core sample of the state at the dawn of the automobile era. A sample that tells you where the edge of town of used to be, where people used to want to go, where the trees started again.

As a result, U.S. 1 is the familiar backdoor to a hundred Florida towns. Past dinky hotels, junkyards, converted fruit stands, and ghosts of former tourist attractions. I squint and slow down to try to see it that way, and you'd be amazed at what a trained eye can find.

It's the longest long way home I know.

July 2004

3 The five seasons of the Darwinian Gardener

"People who say Florida has no seasons have it all wrong. There are five: spring, summer, ultrasummer, fallish, and winterish."

—*The Darwinian Gardener's Almanac*

Air potato vine. (Manipulated Polaroid by Mark Lane)

Spring

Spring tempts people who should not attempt anything more complicated than placing a potted plant on a kitchen windowsill into digging up their yards in misguided garden adventures. That's why the Darwinian Gardener is here. Seek his counsel before giving in to the intoxication of spring.

The Darwinian Gardener advocates survival-of-the-fittest gardening. He does not pick winners or losers. His job is mainly to cart away the bodies of the latter. He is an advocate of zeroscaping. And he's here to answer your questions.

Q: Don't you mean "xeriscaping"?

No, I mean zeroscaping. "Xeriscaping" is maintaining a yard with the least amount of water. Zeroscaping is the science of maintaining a yard with zero work. The principles of xeriscaping work well with zeroscaping. But not when you have to start hauling rocks and boulders around. Moving rocks and splitting boulders are what people do in bad prison movies, and the Darwinian Gardener will have no truck with that.

Q: When is the best time to deal with leaves?

When it gets hard to find your newspaper in the morning. If your newspaper carrier throws a good slider, morning editions can burrow under leaves like something that's alive. It can take days to find them.

Q: What are the best tools for dealing with leaf pileup?

The Darwinian Gardener considers leaf blowers immoral and obnoxious. They are sure evidence that you are using too much firepower and noise in a futile attempt to keep nature at bay. No, the Darwinian Gardener uses only a rake and gloves.

Rakes should be as wide as possible to conserve your effort. Buy a metal one so it will break and rust. This forces you into a trip to the hardware store to buy a new one, and, factoring in the side errands since you're already in the car, you can count on eating up an entire Saturday.

For gloves, I recommend a good, heavy-duty goatskin pair. Leather is the preferred material for its insulation value. Adequately chilled cans of beer are vital to any leaf-raking project, and your fingers will get cold if you use cheap cotton gardening gloves.

The trick is to start raking after the last leaf falls. If you rake before then, it can be just too demoralizing when a single rainstorm undoes minutes and minutes of work. It's enough to make you put on your heaviest-duty garden gloves and head to the refrigerator.

Q: *The homeowners' association is going to hear about you and make your life a living hell.*

That's not a question. And besides, the Darwinian Gardener avoids homeowner associations and places that have been landscaped with bulldozers within the past decade.

Q: *Are lawn gnomes in keeping with the Darwinian Gardener philosophy?*

This is a matter of intense debate within the Darwinian gardening community. There is a slippery-slope argument against gnomes and related species. Once you put up a lawn gnome, you will be tempted to edge and cut and weed to keep it visible. On the other hand, each gnome and frog and flamingo in a yard is a spot that you don't have to mow. And doesn't that count for something?

It goes without saying that in keeping with the principles of zeroscaping, lawn gnomes are acceptable only if unpainted and bought with an eye toward looking quaintly weathered. Painting anything that lives outdoors is too much effort to contemplate.

Q: *Does the Darwinian Gardener feed the birds?*

The Darwinian Gardener feeds the squirrels. It cuts out the middleman.

March 2001

The Darwinian Gardener on tough-love gardening

The Darwinian Gardener paused to lie on the rooftop, Snoopy-style. The roof terrifies the Darwinian Gardener. He sees himself rolling off like an errant fly ball.

The Darwinian Gardener was lying there collecting himself during a particularly vigorous round of roof raking. Friend of the oak tree that he is, the Darwinian Gardener must venture onto the roof with a rake a few times a year to deal with leaf buildup. Leaf buildup is not a big problem, but the stuff rots, and soon you're looking at a spreading brown spot on the ceiling.

Thus the rake. Thus the danger. The Darwinian Gardener is no stranger to personal peril. He laughs at danger. Ha-ha! He is attuned to nature's casual brutality. He knows nobody should approach the fray assuming he's the fittest creature just because he has a plastic rake and opposable thumbs. In the end, the leaves always win. And he can live with that.

The conscientious reader might, at this point, ask, "Who is this Darwinian Gardener? And what about his dark, mysterious past?"

Good point, conscientious reader! I don't know why people say all those things about you.

The Darwinian Gardener practices a survival-of-the-fittest lawn-and-gardening philosophy. He is contemptuous of fussy little roses. He goes by the three-free-waterings-and-you're-on-your-own transplantation rule. His is tough-love horticulture.

His lawnmower has no clipping-bag. Assuming it still works. He's never sure of this. Every successful tug of the starter rope is news to him.

With those introductions out of the way, it's time again to Ask the Darwinian Gardener:

Q: I got this leaf blower/mulcher/lawn-vacuum thing as a birthday present. I feel it compromises my Darwinian Gardener status.

The Darwinian Gardener's attitude toward leaf blowers is severe. Their sound has been medically proven to stimulate centers of the primitive brain responsible for yard rage and homicide. The person who gave you this was no friend.

That said, though, a mulcher can be a useful and awe-inspiring device. Less bagging, faster composting, and the drama of spraying little bits of leaves and twigs through the air. The questions are: Are you disciplined enough to draw the line? To mulch, but not to blow? To vacuum the last of a leaf pile but not to crisscross your lawn getting every last leaf?

People think the Darwinian Gardener has adopted his yard philosophy out of simple laziness. Not so. It takes discipline, an ability to make vital distinctions, a sense of the Tao of yard work to live this lifestyle.

Use the mulching setting only, and that only after noon. "With great power must also come great responsibility," to quote the Amazing Spider-Man.

Q: What's "the six-foot-square exercise" that you allude to as though someone would have the slightest clue about what you're talking about?

The six-foot-square exercise is a technique for preventing a homeowner from going over to the dark side. You set out a small area, six feet by six feet for instance, that you will keep perfect and pristine. The grass will be like carpet. The insects at bay. The leaves somewhere else.

When this work makes you utterly miserable, divide the square footage of your lot by thirty-six and multiply your misery by the answer. Yow, that hurts! And that's the pain you'll suffer if you give in to perfectionism. One thing the Darwinian Gardener is very, very good at is not giving in to perfectionism.

April 2002

Shame and guilt can't move the Darwinian Gardener

The lawn-chemical salesman decided neither diplomacy nor science was working. He switched to guilt and shame.

"So . . . what you're telling me is that you're happy leaving your lawn looking like that?"

Obviously he did not know to whom he was speaking. Shame and guilt as motivators to lawn-and-garden care have roughly zero effect on this sales prospect. All the salesman heard was a darkly amused chuckle before the line went dead.

He could not have known that he had just finished talking to the most dubious sales lead he would pursue that year. He was talking to a man who believes in survival-of-the-fittest lawn care. A man who has murdered colonies of chinch bugs by overfeeding them. The caller did not realize he was talking to the Darwinian Gardener.

So if you promise not to attempt to sell him anything, now would be as good a time as any to Ask the Darwinian Gardener:

Q: Have you—from a strictly lawn-and-garden standpoint—no shame at all?

I have more shame than a Florida legislator but not enough to be inconvenient when it's sunny outside. The Darwinian Gardener is very unclear about this whole good/bad thing when it comes to lawn care. He's not a conscientious objector in nature's ongoing war—that's the Transcendental Gardener. (Just follow the annoying tinkle of wind chimes until you find her yard.) Nor is he a Zen gardener who spends hours raking pebbles. No, he is content to watch nature, see how things are lining up, and then pretend he was always with the winning side.

He considers himself something of a Nietzschean gardener working on a yard that's beyond good and evil and free of the petty social conventions that yoke mankind to angry and loud machines powered by small-horsepower gasoline engines.

Q: What impact does your "philosophy" have on all property values within a half-mile radius?

The Darwinian Gardener, of all persons, respects the verdicts of the marketplace. He believes that aside from the virtues of thrift and low water use, his gardening philosophy works well with the real estate market.

People love to gaze upon perfect little gardens and golf course lawns, but they don't always want to live there. Most buyers are properly wary of places that seem to say: "If you're not willing to dedicate your life to maintaining this, you are unworthy of this land."

The marketplace accepts customers as they are. Not as you would like them to be. A too-perfect lawn is a drag on the market; it intimidates buyers. People want to buy places they can improve upon. Not places they can't live up to.

Far from being a drag on the market, the Darwinian gardening philosophy is—to use an economist's buzz phrase merely to sound smart and important—a value-added activity.

Q: Do you ever feel you spend more time and effort devising elaborate explanations for why you don't do work than you would if just did the work?

It's not the number of hours that count, it's the quality.

Q: Why do they call it St. Augustine grass, anyway?

They call it St. Augustine grass because of its inventor.

St. Augustine, as you doubtless already know, had a pretty downbeat outlook on human nature. He knew that, left sitting around wondering what to do on a summer day, people were bound to come up with bad ideas. So he decided to develop something that would require huge amounts of care and resources so people would lavish time, money, and effort on their lawns instead of other, more sinful and destructive activities.

That's also why he invented the weed whacker. I read that on the Internet somewhere, so I'm pretty sure it's true.

Q: How do you deal with fire ant mounds?

I try to build to a trot, but short of a run, before mowing over them with the lawnmower. You get fewer bites that way.

Like a lot of life's problems, there's something to be said for closing your eyes and mowing on ahead as fast as you can.

April 2003

Summer

After so many weeks of unremitting rain, the Darwinian Gardener was getting restless. Finely attuned to the workings of nature, he felt this was too much of a good thing.

His first thought was one of self-censure. It had been a premature and rash act to run the sprinklers, not once but twice, last June with the excuse that this was a drought and an emergency and because he felt bad for the frogs. Now they are far happier than they have any right to be.

But the wind and rain also had the salutary effect of bringing down dead tree limbs that previously had been out of reach. Only last month he had thought vaguely about getting out a ladder and borrowing a long-handled saw to cut them off, but the exertion involved in contemplating such a task was enough to send him inside to lie down.

If you're patient enough, these problems often solve themselves. And, as so often happens, his philosophy paid off.

But we're getting ahead of ourselves. Who is this Darwinian Gardener and what is this "philosophy" he espouses? What is the secret behind his calm acceptance of everything from chinch bugs to tropical storms? And does he really have to dress like that? Good questions all.

The Darwinian Gardener believes in survival-of-the-fittest gardening. His job is to be no more than nature's referee. You introduce the fighters, step back, and see that the losers are carried from the ring.

He is the pal of adaptable native species. He refuses to be an enabler for high-strung, fussy plant life that expects to be catered to and pampered. He refuses to trick plants into thinking they don't really live in coastal Florida.

He achieves a Zen-like calm with the knowledge that most of what happens in his yard isn't his fault. Once you can convincingly blame nature, you have an alibi that lasts for all time.

And yes. He does have to dress like that.

These introductions dispensed with, it's time to Ask the Darwinian Gardener:

Q: I feel helpless watching the rain fall and being unable to do anything about the yard or grass. I can hear it growing. Is there nothing to be done?

Nope, nothing. There are three distinct stages of doing nothing because of rain.

First there's the storm's-a-brewing, anyone-fool-enough-to-be-outside-is-asking-to-be-struck-by-lightning stage. This is the one that holds the most drama.

Then there's the not-fit-outside-for-man-nor-beast stage. This carries the most weight. (Remember: Heavy misting and ultrahumidity count as rain for work-avoidance purposes.)

Finally there's the too-wet-to-do-anything stage. This is the hardest stage to use as a convincing argument, but it can work for days. This kind of wetness can really eat up yard equipment.

Say this with real concern in your voice.

Q: What do I do about the racket the frogs are making after the rain?

Sit back and enjoy it. This is what happens when water, frogs, and sex combine. People buy New Age and Space Music CDs to approximate this kind of calming white noise. By opening the windows, you can get the same effect without expense, stereo equipment, or the ridicule of others.

All of natural creation boogies with the slacking of a drought. I think this is one more thing we can learn from nature.

Q: All of a sudden, all these mushrooms are appearing all over the place. Is there any sure rule for telling poisonous from nonpoisonous mushrooms?

Yes, there is. The nonpoisonous ones are wrapped in cellophane or are on top of pizza. Some say they come in cans, too, but the Darwinian Gardener is skeptical.

July 2002

Ultrasummer

Many people ask the Darwinian Gardener about insects. Particularly mosquitoes. And not in a nice way, either. In a sneering, gotcha-now way.

You may have noticed that after more than a month of near-daily rains, the mosquito population has returned with its old vigor. The drought had kept them in line for a long time. Now that they're back, everybody acts amazed that swarms of biting insects live here.

But we're getting ahead of ourselves. Who is this man who has achieved the serenity of someone who gardens like nobody's looking and waters like it's going to hurt?

Good question. The Darwinian Gardener is an adherent of survival-of-the-fittest gardening. He nudges plant life along, stands back, and watches natural forces duke it out. Not only does he not take sides in the natural struggle, he quotes with approval the rascally, abrasive title character of the film *The Royal Tenenbaums*, who shouts from the roof: "There are no sides!"

Still, the latest swarming of mosquitoes and the nasty backlash it has caused have forced him to open the floor to questions. It's time once again to Ask the Darwinian Gardener:

Q: Well, Mr. Natural-Hippy-Dippy-Tree-Hugger-Don't-Use-Pesticides, what are you doing now that you're being eaten alive by mosquitoes, huh? I bet you're bombing your yard with clouds of advanced chemicals, aren't you? Your kind always folds in a natural disaster.

Well, Mr. Spray-and-Bomb-Outdoor-Control-Freak, the Darwinian Gardener doesn't much like your tone.

The Darwinian Gardener lives in a community that was named Mosquito County in the 19th century. Old Spanish maps identify the area with names like Mosquito Inlet, Mosquito River, Los Mosquitos and variants. This suggests a problem that is not to be solved in one trip to the hardware store.

The Darwinian Gardener is convinced the only reason he stopped growing at five feet ten inches (rounded up to the nearest whole number) is the cumulative chemical effect of riding a bicycle behind the Volusia County Mosquito Control District fogging truck.

What was the appeal in riding through that stuff? The smell? The surreal sense of riding through clouds?

A bad idea, regardless.

Q: *In keeping with the Darwinian Gardener philosophy, what kind of a repellent do you use on your porch or hammock?*

The Darwinian Gardener seldom worries about being repellent enough. Effectively channeling that quality is the only problem.

His favorite mosquito repellent is, unfortunately, also an effective people repellent—cheap cigars. They keep bugs away, they keep people away, but they don't seem to bother the dog much.

The Darwinian Gardener also uses citronella candles and like products. Whether they work or not, he does not know. He just likes the smell. It takes him back to growing up in Florida.

And it's the only insect repellent used in tiki torches. Why can't other helpful chemicals be dispensed like that?

Q: *How do citronella candles work?*

Here's the Darwinian Gardener's theory about citronella candles—they don't actually keep mosquitoes away, but when you inhale the fumes, they stimulate the don't-care centers of your brain. This makes the bugs just another thing you can live with. That's why you wake up the next morning wondering how you got all those bites.

Q: *Since when did the don't-care centers of your brain ever require stimulation?*

A different sort of outdoor/garden writer would take umbrage at many of the inquiries the Darwinian Gardener must deal with.

July 2002

Hurricane season

The Darwinian Gardener surveyed his yard after Hurricane Charley and estimated the supplies required for a job this size. Easily, it would take four cigars and a six-pack of an amber domestic beer; anything heavier might impede his progress.

The Darwinian Gardener is a big believer in careful job preparation and site surveying. He does not jump into things like this higgledy-piggledy. There is much to consider.

Hurricane Charley had presented him with a bona fide yard disaster. And while many people consider the normal condition of his lawn to be a bona fide yard disaster, this was something of an altogether different magnitude.

But wait, who is this natural philosopher of yard and field? Who is this homeowner skilled in all ways of contending with Florida's overactive nature? Who is this man who considers days without electric power to be "like camping except you know where your stuff is?"

The Darwinian Gardener is a man who believes in survival-of-the-fittest lawn care. He shrugs off the fall of mighty oaks and won't play favorites with flora. He is unsentimental about the inability of cedars to cope with adversity. He won't be drawn into a losing game each time a bush or fussy little flowering plant loses its zest for life.

And in time of lawn disaster, you could do a lot worse than to Ask the Darwinian Gardener:

Q: What's with this "site survey" piffle? It sounds more like straight-up procrastination.

The Darwinian Gardener understands that staying motivated is the most important part of the job. You have to prepare yourself psychologically or the job will never get done.

Then you have to figure out where public safety and landscape aesthetics demand action. Plus you have to designate your rough patch.

Q: What's a "rough patch?"

That's the spot you don't touch until the job is almost over. It's a living "before" picture. Something you can point to and say, "Hey, at least the whole yard doesn't look like that." You need it to feel as though you've made any progress after an hour.

Q: Yeah, then what?

Next, you set priorities:

First is the path out of the house and driveway.

Second is the biggest, nastiest downed tree or branch.

Third is the area that most depresses you.

Fourth, the area that most impresses or depresses the average on-looker.

With the work order set, you'll soon be doing the lawn debris shuffle.

Q: What is "the lawn debris shuffle?" Does it look as dumb as it sounds?

The lawn debris shuffle is performed when you move across the yard in a sliding, shuffling motion, not picking your feet up much, until a ball of twigs and branches and leaves grows in front of you. Rakes aren't made for this situation.

The Darwinian Gardener is convinced that this is better aerobic exercise than Pilates. And definitely low-impact. Low-impact is his kind of impact. Like all exercise, it looks dumb but is worth the effort.

The Darwinian Gardener is in discussions about a video and book project on this, but has not yet found a taker.

Q: I bulldozed, cut, and poisoned every tree and sprig of a bush in front of my house to get the perfect, blandly featureless lawn. Tree debris don't bother me. Haw-haw, tree-hugger!

The owner of an oak grove pays for it with every fifteen-year storm. The owner of a perfect lawn suffers every weekend. And that is how the Darwinian Gardener prefers to live—on the edge, a life of unpredictable danger. He's that kind of guy.

August 2004

Late hurricane season

The Darwinian Gardener enjoys the hearty *thwack* sound of an ax upon log. He just wishes the cuts wouldn't land so far apart. He does not have the best eye for a clean cut. Although this year he has been improving.

In this month after the storms, while his neighborhood echoes with the sounds of chain saws, leaf blowers, and other wonders of the two-stroke engine, he is appreciating anew the usefulness of unpowered hand tools. Renewing long rusty skills.

Thwick! And the branch flies apart in two directions. He rests the handle on his shoulder, looks out to the distance, and strikes a pose before picking up the pieces.

A good ax not only can get the job done faster than a saw, but more important, you look good using it. Which, as we all know, is vital in an image-conscious age.

This isn't mere gardening, it's connecting with the American woodsman myth. Abe Lincoln or Fess Parker as depicted in the tableau on a metal Daniel Boone lunch box. That sort of thing.

But wait. Who is this primitive figure using a crude wedge and brute force in the age of cordless lawn equipment? The Darwinian Gardener is an advocate of survival-of-the-fittest gardening. He is unsentimental about the plants that ate it during the storms. What's down, he cuts up. What's broken, he cuts back. He wishes he had photographed his two-story yard-debris pile because it was the most impressive feature his yard ever boasted.

When planning your post-storm landscaping, it can't hurt too much to Ask the Darwinian Gardener:

Q: I'm planting trees to replace those that have fallen. But I forget: are laurel oaks the bad oaks and live oaks the good? Or the other way around?

The Darwinian Gardener is always unclear about this whole good/bad thing. He was looking picturesque chopping wood last week because The Tree Guy had cut down a laurel oak that had been leaning over his roof like an angry, tilting, inverted "L." There are no bad trees. But there are a few—a minority to be sure—that want to kill you, crush your house, and get your CD collection out of order. Sadly, these are often laurel oaks.

Q: So how do I tell the difference between different kinds of oaks when I replant?

Here's the Darwinian Gardener's rule of thumb: plant whatever looks like the stuff already growing well on your soil. Just be sure to sell your house and move someplace else within twenty years. Like children, oaks take a long time to get big and become dangers to life and property. Twenty years is plenty of time to get out of the way after you've planted the wrong tree.

Q: *What decorative plant best weathers hurricane seasons?*

The Darwinian Gardener recommends banana trees for the sense of drama they lend.

After tropical storms and hurricanes, their leaves look shredded to pieces and droopy, and the whole plant looks about to die. Three weeks later they look great. After freezes they look discolored and droopy and about to die. Then three weeks later they're back again.

There are no minor setbacks for a banana tree. Everything's a Big Deal. They overreact to all setbacks and then look as good as new if you just ignore them.

There are great life lessons to be learned here, but the Darwinian Gardener is not one to name names.

October 2004

Fallish

Spring forward; fall back. Twice a year the Darwinian Gardener repeats the daylight-saving time mnemonic. Spring forward: move the clock up. Lose an hour of sleep. Wake up in the dark. Fall back: move the clock back. Sleep an hour later. Make dinner in the dark.

The Darwinian Gardener is not a morning person and greatly favors the autumn time change. It puts society on a biorhythm closer to his own. The spring time shift, conversely, causes him naught but suffering.

"Fall back" also summarizes his approach to autumn gardening. A time of fallow fields and lawns that can go untouched for another weekend, sparing his lawn from the dull blow of his mower's blades.

But wait, the aware citizen might object, who is this person who presumes to be the armchair critic of time, seasons, and nature? Good question, aware citizen. You are as awake and touchy as ever.

The Darwinian Gardener is a person who believes in survival-of-the-fittest gardening. No cosseting drooping flowers that were planted as souvenirs from foreign climes. No chemical warfare against the enemies of plants that refuse to stand up for themselves. He is nature's fair-weather fan, declaring only for the odds-on favorites and putting his money on obvious winners.

And since he does even less work outside in the fall than in other months, this is the best time of year to Ask the Darwinian Gardener:

Q: Why does the Darwinian Gardener have so much time on his hands in fall? Isn't this the most wonderful time of the year for holiday outdoor decorations?

The Darwinian Gardener is a natural philosopher and his expertise does not reach to the handiwork of man. But since you asked:

Outdoor home decoration is one of those great two-kinds-of-people questions. A task that one part of the population undertakes cheerfully, even with a degree of unquestioning anticipation, while the other part regards it with incomprehension seasoned with the bitter spice of dread. He tends toward the latter, considering this a dangerous comingling of the labor-intensive elements of craft work and landscaping.

Just contemplating it makes him want to go inside and lie down.

Q: I am shopping for mailboxes and am looking at one of the sweet manatee-holding-a-mailbox varieties. What do you recommend?

Although this is a yard question, it rather falls out of the Darwinian Gardener's area of expertise. That said, he has a fondness for the lawn art you describe. He was, however, witness to a friend's manatee mailbox holder being savagely scarred by a boat trailer as it backed out of his driveway.

It taught him that even on dry land, these creatures have natural enemies.

Q: You make yourself out to be such an expert and all, so why did you claim that you could plant pieces of Halloween candy corn to grow candy corn stalks? All I got was a lot of ants, and my wife laughed at me. Where's the correction?

The Darwinian Gardener feels your pain. The number one enemy of candy-corn plants are ants and roaches. The kernels are prone to mold and melting, too.

That's why they're nearly impossible to grow in Florida. Look on the bags and you will find that all the stuff is imported from out of state.

I suspect you either tried to plant the Indian corn variety, which everyone knows won't grow, or planted the entire kernel. I've been told you should plant only the tips. And even then they are tricky to cultivate. That's what I've read on Wikipedia, anyway.

Good luck!

October 2003

Fallish II

The Darwinian Gardener paused in his labors to aim the lawn mower. Fall mowing is a trickier proposition than in summer. In August, he leaves clear paths through six-inch-high grass. Now, the growth is spotty and only the sandspurs give a clear guide.

The Darwinian Gardener abhors wasted effort. And on a weekend, he's not that big on regular effort, either. So he lines up his path with a sharp eye.

But stop and set the choke to idle. Who is this Darwinian Gardener, and what's he doing behind a mower just before the twin holidays of Halloween and Election Day?

The Darwinian Gardener is America's foremost advocate of survival-of-the-fittest lawn- and garden-care. He knows that he's not the director of nature's show; he's just the theater's landlord who counts the take and is baffled at each season's offerings.

And before you overreact to the first cool snap of the season, you should Ask the Darwinian Gardener. And then you can overreact.

Q: So why are you mowing before your grass has gone to seed?

As a public service, the Darwinian Gardener feels he should minimize the damage that sandspurs do to the costuming of trick-or-treaters. Besides, this is the last time he expects to be mowing this calendar year, so he wants to use up the gas in the mower. He usually stays on the job until the thing sputters and stops on its own. Also, timely mowing allows him to keep clear paths through the sword fern in the Experimental Garden.

Q: What the heck is this Experimental Garden you talk about?

This is a section of his backyard that he has allowed to grow wild with even less intervention or supervision than the rest of his yard. The turtles, snakes, and armadillos seem to particularly like it. Although this is a hands-off precinct of his yard, the sword fern is so ferocious that the Darwinian Gardener feels threatened and must prove that he, not it, is the dominant life form in these here parts.

He calls it the Experimental Garden because he carefully observes what shows up there. Sometimes he'll even rescue something pretty from that part of the yard and put it out front. Anyway, the name sounds better and has more economy of expression than calling it the Part of the Yard I Won't Do Anything to Except Randomly Mow Down Sword Fern.

Q: Does anything other than sword fern, old world climbing fern, and things with stickers and thorns grow in that godforsaken patch of ground?

Yes! The plant known as the beautyberry grows there, too. The beautyberry (*Callicarpa americana*) is a most excellent plant. It's native to Florida. It resists being planted on purpose and tends to grow where it wants to grow. The Darwinian Gardener respects that.

It looks stunning half the year, unexceptional a quarter of the year, and flat-out dead a quarter of the year.

At the base of its leaves, sometime in late fall, it grows thick clusters of tiny berries the color of summer-camp fruit punch. Birds attack them greedily.

This is a volunteer plant in the Experimental Garden. This means it has a much better attitude than the draftees, which are often unprepared for the rigors before them.

Q: Where did you get those realistic-looking spider webs that greet trick-or-treaters at your front door?

They've been there since the spiders made them in August. You should see the very scary laundry room!

October 2006

Winterish

This was, he had to admit, a thing of strange beauty. The Darwinian Gardener slowed his car to take it in. He was driving past a yard where each palm tree and most bigger plants had been wrapped in form-fitting jackets of bed sheets and beach towels secured with bungee cords and triple-wrapped twine.

On an afternoon before an expected freeze, you usually see more slap-dash protection. Something that looks like an explosion in a coin-laundry. But this must have taken hours to create.

Seen as art, it looked like an intriguing statement about natural form and the doomed quest to control the natural world. Seen as garden maintenance, it looked like a lot of work. Unnecessary, if too warm. Futile, if too cold.

But wait. Who is this mysterious driver talking like a lawn and art critic? Who is this backyard outdoorsman who claims he doesn't need a weatherman to tell which way the wind blows? Who is this Darwinian Gardener?

The Darwinian Gardener believes in survival-of-the-fittest gardening. He is not nature's over-solicitous waiter. He is more like the guy in a paper hat handing out bags at nature's takeout window. And he won't give out ketchup packets unless they're demanded of him. And even then only after looking the customer over in an appraising manner.

As this area warms after its sort-of near-freeze, you can't be blamed for wanting to Ask the Darwinian Gardener:

Q: *So what do you do when you hear about a freeze, Mr. Too-Cool-to-Stir-from-Your-Barcalounger-and-Bundle-Bougainvillea?*

The Darwinian Gardener sees cold snaps as part of the natural cycle. But people who move to Florida often feel betrayed and hurt when they discover that winter happens here. If he might engage in cheap psycho-analysis, the Darwinian Gardener believes these newcomers project their alarm onto their plants.

Because Florida weather doesn't change much day to day, the Darwinian Gardener pays little attention to weather reports except in hurricane season. If he notices laundry in other people's yards, he'll dig his sweater out of a box and bring potted plants inside.

Q: *So you don't wrap your plants?*

No, the whole plant-wrapping thing seems out of the spirit of Darwinian gardening. You can't plant as though it's Miami and expect to get away with it forever. This is a hard lesson. One that plant wrapping can put off only so long.

The Darwinian Gardener is always impressed at the way unwrapped hibiscus, ficus, and banana trees bounce back from near-death experiences. He likes to think their brushes with death give them an appreciation for life and a stronger will to survive.

Q: And you apply this to your precious orange tree, too?

Don't speak disrespectfully of my poor, wind-wounded orange tree! It's among the oldest citrus trees in my ZIP code. I feel an obligation to it.

Much as Shinto priests plant small ceremonial rice patches as a living connection with an ancient and virtuous past, so, too is backyard citrus exempt from the hardy precepts of Darwinian gardening. It is a mystic totem of Old Florida.

As such, yes, it is wrapped with a beach towel during the harshest multi-evening freezes. I draw the line, though, at using any chemical whose name I have to sound out upon reading.

Q: When will the dead branches from the 2004 hurricanes finally stop falling on my roof?

Around the time the dead branches from the 2005 hurricanes *start* falling on your roof.

June 2004

Darwinian Gardener versus the air potato

The Darwinian Gardener's bucket was half full. And it did not denote an optimistic temperament. He was doing his postfreeze chores.

This is light duty consisting mainly of carrying off the dead and cautiously calculating the odds on the near-dead. And, too, walking around the backyard, eyes on the dirt, and carrying a bucket. This is an annual event.

Every February he fills a bucket with the hard, bizarrely misshapen, mean-looking seeds of the dreaded air-potato vine. They are mostly the size of billiard balls.

He is occasionally amused to find one with a pair of tiny teeth marks, showing where a squirrel had taken an exploratory nibble and spat the thing out. Even these most undiscriminating of rodents have no use for air potatoes.

Every year he is amazed at how fast the bucket fills. Every year he congratulates himself at successfully fighting the good fight. Yet every year he finds himself back doing the same thing.

But hold that thought. Who is this Darwinian Gardener, and what dark secrets lie hidden beneath his deceptively tranquil exterior?

The Darwinian Gardener is a backyard natural philosopher who believes in survival-of-the-fittest garden-and-lawn care. He is not nature's cop. He is nature's inattentive referee, blowing his whistle only when there's blood on the foul line. And not always then.

And once again, it's time to Ask the Darwinian Gardener:

Q: If you're so Darwinian and everything, why are you going after a vine like it's some big deal?

A reasonable question, though I'm not sure I like your tone of voice.

The air-potato vine (*Dioscorea bulbifer*) is a non-native, invasive vine found everywhere in Florida. It is unnoticeable in spring but by late summer blocks the sun, chokes trees, and threatens to envelope particularly lazy dogs.

The Darwinian Gardener generally agrees with Ralph Waldo Emerson that a weed is "a plant whose virtues have never been discovered." (Or, to update the sentiment, a plant without an ad agency.) But the air potato goes far beyond being a weed. It wants to take over the planet. And we, in Florida, Polynesia and West Africa are mankind's first lines of defense.

Q: Do you really believe these are some kind of alien life form bent on the destruction of humanity?

Of course not, silly. I think they were originally *planted* by alien life forms bent on the destruction of humanity.

I'm not some kind of kook.

Q: Why do they keep coming back?

Oftentimes newcomers to the state think these vines look kind of pretty and jungle-like and marvel at their ability to hide any rusted or broken-down fence under a luxuriant coat of shiny, spade-shaped leaves.

The thought comes into their heads, seemingly from out of nowhere: *Maybe I should help these things grow. They're so pretty.*

This is mind control of the most simple alien-plant variety. You'd think people would have learned by now.

Q: What sort of herbicide should I use?

The Darwinian Gardener is flexible, but not that flexible. If you're not in this for the long haul, if you reach for a bottle of chemicals every time an alien usurper invades your yard, if you're not willing to collect ugly, potato-like seeds occasionally, you might as well put down your rake and buy a condo overlooking a parking lot somewhere.

The Darwinian Gardener knows that flashy short-term solutions are often futile, sometimes counterproductive, and always a whole lot of effort. At the risk of sounding like a NATO foreign minister, he believes in containment and is wary of preemptive strikes.

February 2003.

4 In NASCAR's backyard

"My favorite race is the Rolex 24 Hours, the one where cars go around for twenty-four hours and whichever one doesn't blow up or crash wins. Like business, politics, life, and evolutionary biology—you gotta be there at the end."

—*The Darwinian Gardener's Almanac*

Illustration by Bruce Beattie.

Romance and racin' tempestuously fall
into each other's arms

I'm still trying to get my mind around the announcement, made earlier this month, that NASCAR and the foremost publisher of romance novels, Harlequin Enterprises, are putting out a series of racing romances. It's not that I can't imagine My Little Town as a backdrop to romance, passion, and the stuff of the flea market's three-books-for-a-buck tables. But I must admit it's not easy.

This is probably nothing more than a result of overfamiliarity. I'm sure we can, too, be the kind of romantic locale where eyes lock, bosoms heave, and lives change on the spot.

Instead of walking up the castle parapet, the characters could go up in the Daytona Beach Pier's Space Needle. Or something. Instead of the mansion on the moor, there's the Speedway skyboxes. And how different are they really?

I'm sure the possibilities are endless.

✳

His words were interrupted when the garage reverberated from an engine's sudden backfire. The explosion took Lorna-Sue's breath away.

"Is that a Chevy 5.3-liter LS4 Small-Block V-8 engine with variable valve timing?" she asked herself.

"Or is it . . . my heart!"

✳

Still, the obstacles are formidable. Remember: unlike baseball, football, and even horse racing, there has never been a good racing movie. Not even the ones with Elvis or Tom Cruise. Do sellers of swoon really think they can succeed where Elvis and Tom Cruise have failed?

I don't know what mitigates against a racing movie. Is it the go-fast, turn-left simplicity of races? A certain yee-haw factor of the infield?

The answer may be more mundane—the inescapable reality of track noise. This kills any dialogue during races.

✳

In the night infield, halfway through the Rolex 24 Hours of Daytona, Junior could stand it no longer. The headlights of a nearby RV lit up her blonde hair and made her look just as she had when she still worked for Lopez Cams.

"I love you Virginia-Raye. I loved you from that first photo shoot when you

posed with me in a purple thong and a 'Miss Overhead Cam 2002' sash. Then you were just arm-candy for when we schmoozed the sponsors. But now, now you mean so much more to me."

"You say somethin', Junior?"

"I said, 'I love you Virginia-Raye. I loved you from that first photo shoot . . .'"

"Junior, I'm going to have to take these ear protectors off. I see your lips are movin'. That's about it."

"I said . . . "

"You say you need another beer, honey? Is that it? You know where the damn cooler is."

✳

Then there's the whole sponsorship problem. How do you write about races without giving away free advertising? You can't ignore it because it's integral to the sport. And yet there's something unromantic about the whole product-endorsement thing.

✳

Jimbo staggered from the hubbub of the winner's circle, unsteady on his legs and half suspecting it would all turn out to be a dream. Lorelei-Sue noticed that his orange jumpsuit was now half unzipped, emphasizing his broad shoulders, revealing his manly, chiseled chest, and separating the syllables of his sponsor's name silk-screened across the front.

SUD . . . ZEE it said now.

"Hey, Lorelei-Sue," he said. "You feelin' okay?"

She felt her knees go wobbly. "It's just, that, that . . . well, Sudzee's been my detergent every since I was a little girl. It brings so much back . . ."

"Whew, good save," she thought.

✳

I suppose I'll just have to wait for titles like *The Heart Knows No Restrictor Plate*, *Driveshaft of Passion*, and *Four-Barrel Love* before I'll get to see how these delicate questions are handled.

December 2005

When did bumps turn to slams?

Media critics have urged the nation's journalists to stop dwelling on obvious non-stories like a vice president of the United States shooting somebody and instead address the Real Issues Facing America. Good advice. Which is why it's time to face the bump-drafting issue.

In stock-car racing, bump-drafting is when a car drafting behind a lead car bumps it squarely in back, allowing both cars to go faster. Drafting—if you really don't follow this sort of thing—is the way cars line up behind leaders in drafting lines. The car in front pushes through the air resistance in front of it, and that makes it easier for the car immediately behind. But the car running behind also helps the car in front by breaking up the low-pressure air behind it. Result: both cars go faster than they would alone. That's why you get the stirring sight of strings of cars running close together for maximum aerodynamic advantage.

Drivers must make and shift drafting-line alliances in a race and make split-second judgments about how to time this. Which is where the whole drive-fast, turn-left view of racing breaks down. Bump-drafting is a harsh refinement of usual drafting tactics. Except that if a lot of drivers are doing it at 190 mph—some with more finesse than others—things can get dangerous. Who could have guessed?

Defending Nextel Cup champion Tony Stewart came out and said so with his own mouth Sunday and was quickly seconded by other drivers. NASCAR then announced it would police "unnecessary" bump-drafting, admittedly a pretty subjective call.

I work within earshot of the Speedway (okay, everybody in town works within earshot of the Speedway), and I don't recall hearing the term *bump-drafting* before last year. Much less its new variant, *slam-drafting*. (As in: "Bump-drafting is just racin'. Now, slam-drafting; that's dangerous.")

Looking in the *Daytona Beach News-Journal*'s library database, the earliest mention of "bump-drafting" appeared February 14, 1999. It must not have been a new term then because it was used without any further explanation: "Andy Hillenburg triggered the upside slide by trying to bump-draft [Casey] Atwood and push Atwood ahead of race leader Randy LaJoie." (The *New York Times* used the term in 1988 but treated it as a strictly truck-racing phenomenon.)

It could be argued that *bump-drafting* is a refinement of *love tap*, a term that has been used from time immemorial, which is to say, before the 1990s. But while some bump-drafts are love taps, not all love taps are bump-drafts.

Got that?

Bump-drafting appeared in no more than four stories a year in the *News-Journal* through 2004. Then in 2005, it jumped to fifteen stories. This year the term has already appeared in nine stories. The refinement, *slam-drafting*, gained popularity last year.

If, even in sports writing, language mirrors life, then something changed last year. And what appears to have changed is that the practice became harder, more widespread, and less skillfully applied than in the past.

From love tap to bump-draft to slam-draft. I'm still waiting for the phrase *extreme maximum atomic slam-draft* to appear.

Because everybody knows racing is a metaphor for life, the universe, and everything, the whole bump-draft/slam-draft controversy raises again an age-old question: when does a competitive situation get so competitive and hard-fought that the game itself is endangered?

This gets asked beyond sports—in politics, in business, in law. Anywhere that winners and losers sort themselves out. So maybe this is less a reflection on stock-car racing than on our own slam-draft era.

At least when push comes to slam.

February 2006

3

In front of Daytona International Speedway, two days after the Daytona 500, work crews are sweeping up, and a trickle of Dale Earnhardt race fans are mourning at the fountain in front of the track. Beneath a larger-than-life statue of Big Bill France, the late founder of NASCAR, people are leaving votive candles, roses, black toy race cars, and expressions of grief written on pretty much anything with a flat surface and the number 3.

On a flap of corrugated cardboard, laid beneath a plastic checkered flag with a "3" Sharpie-scrawled in each white square, somebody wrote, "My 10 yrs. old son said who are we going to root for now? That ripped my heart out. We love you Dale."

Trying to explain the impact of Dale Earnhardt's death to someone not around auto racing, someone from out of town, is not easy. There are no analogies in the outside world. Certainly nothing equivalent in other sports. The last baseball death was in 1920; NASCAR lost three drivers last season.

Driving 180 mph in close formation is a dangerous way to make a living. A racing driver needs the reflexes of a fighter pilot, the nerves of a bomb-disposal technician, and the mental stamina of a marathon runner. And most people don't consider them athletes because all they do is sit in a car.

Earnhardt, however, was "The Intimidator," and the danger was only to mortals. He had won a top ten position in four hundred and four races, won thirty-four races at Daytona International Speedway and had been racing twenty-five years.

If Hollywood had the wit to create a good racing movie—something that so far has eluded it—nobody could write a more stunning end.

Listen: there's this racing legend. He's at the peak of his career. And it's the last lap of the big race. This is his track. The one where he's won more races than anyone. And he's driving deliberately to protect the leads of his son and this other driver. One who works for him and has to break a losing streak that's been dogging him for years. Then, within yards of the spot where his best friend had died back in the third reel, something goes horribly wrong.

Freeze frame. Fade to black.

The next day, all around town, people spontaneously lowered house flags to half staff. Banners with Earnhardt's Number 3 logo, its familiar black background now all too fitting, were somberly hung in front of homes and businesses.

Most of the day there was a line thirty deep out the door of the *Daytona Beach News-Journal's* office and snaking into the parking lot. Race fans trying to buy newspapers with the crash on the front page. Every rack in town had been picked clean, and people were desperate to have a piece of that day. It's hard to explain this to someone from out of town.

Earnhardt was a transitional figure in racing. He had one foot in racing's good-ol'-boy, drive-hard-and-leave-your-paint- on-the-other-guy's-fender past and the other in the promotionally savvy, worldwide-audience, multimedia present.

He appealed to both new and longtime race fans. That translated into a lot of Number 3 T-shirts, mugs, and jackets and lured sponsors.

Still, unlike photogenic younger drivers like Jeff Gordon, he often looked a bit stiff, out of place, waving frosting-filled cookies or holding sodas in life-size cardboard-cutout supermarket advertising displays, and you had to like him for that. Maybe it was the smile. The one that might be friendly or might be a threat. You could never quite tell. You were glad you didn't have to.

Still, if his marketing was state-of-the-art New NASCAR, the Earnhardt racing style was refined Old School. Calculating, aggressive, consistent, and fearless.

Who do you root for now? And if you do, which race, which lap, will be the one that will break your heart next time?

This isn't like a rock star dying in a plane crash or a sports star expiring off camera. The sport and the field are now different. And there are only mortals left at the starting line.

February 2001

Deep Thinker finds life, politics, business, and netwar are a lot like racing

Racin' is a lot like life. This is a truism I've heard over many beers and lots of years. And like most truisms, it wouldn't be a truism if it weren't, well, mostly true.

I have a new reason to believe this courtesy of David Ronfeldt, a senior social scientist with RAND Corporation. Ronfeldt's job is explaining complex social phenomena such as how the Internet has transformed society, how societies organize themselves, and how international politics work. Heavy stuff. "I work on the implications of the information revolution on the future of conflict and cooperation," he says modestly.

Like many deep thinkers, Ronfeldt also is a NASCAR fan. He describes himself as "part egg-head, part rev-head."

After watching Jeff Gordon's dramatic win in the 1999 Daytona 500—taking the lead in the 190th lap and holding off Dale Earnhardt for 10 hard-fought laps—it occurred to Ronfeldt that racing is a lot like life. Like political alliances, like business strategy, like a lot of complex social structures.

"I was already doing work involving network analysis and complexity theory and the connections were just automatically apparent to me," he said. "I just started writing the paper."

The paper, "Social Science at 190 mph on NASCAR's Biggest Super-speedways," appeared two years ago in the Internet academic journal "First Monday."

In that '99 season, Ronfeldt said he saw what a lot of fans see— "because of partnering, you could go faster." He says these fluid, spur-of-the-moment partnerships make big-track stock car racing the first postmodern sport.

But let's back up here and explain a little racing. When a car roars around a racetrack, it must push its way through the air in front of it and leave a vacuum in its wake. The high-pressure air in front of the car slows it down. The low-pressure air behind the car also slows it down.

When another car pulls behind a leader, both cars can go faster. The low-pressure drag on the leader is diminished by the second car. The second car can go faster because it doesn't have to fight high-pressure air in front of it. Both cars benefit.

That's why you see lines of cars following each other closely. It's called drafting. Drivers win by making quick strategic alliances. A driver who doesn't draft and tries to run alone is fighting physics.

"Stock car racing, at its highest levels, reflects an important, desirable American trait: How to compete by doing a good job at cooperating," Ronfeldt writes.

Think about it. When Microsoft and Intel say they're cooperating on a product launch, isn't that like drafting? Each is working off the movement of the other, and either will peel off the second a new opening appears. Likewise, as executives move up the corporate ladder, they draft behind shifting frontrunners, planning to move out on the backstretch.

During NATO's war in Kosovo, Ronfeldt writes, wasn't Great Britain drafting in the lead of the United States? This made both more formidable and left less room for critics of the war, such as France and Russia, to form another draft line. Both were left hung out to dry.

And in fighting terrorism, says Ronfeldt, "The CIA and FBI need to form a drafting relationship and behave more like Daytona and less like Bristol."

If football is compared to old-fashioned combat, then the Pepsi 400 is more like "netwar." Netwar, a word Ronfeldt helped coin, describes how small, decentralized groups link up in social conflicts. "It's a mode of conflict using network forms of organization either for good purposes or bad purposes," he says. Like racing, this conflict is "nonhierarchical and self-organizing."

The article concludes: "These few examples—and others that wait to be identified—suggest that a new range of social science theory might be developed around the concept or metaphor of the long draft line. They also suggest—that, in short, much of life is like a Daytona-type race."

Like we always said.

July 2002

Nextel Cup Series a mouthful of change

The biggest problem with the NASCAR-Nextel deal is all those consonants. The Southern mouth likes consonants that don't demand a lot of exertion of tongue, tooth and cheek. It likes syllables that glide into each other. Instead, the "x" in the telecom company's name acts as a hard roadblock. A sign that says, "Stop right there, buddy. Come to a complete stop before proceeding to the next syllable." But heck, for $700 million, Southern mouths can be retrained.

The deal between Nextel Communications, a wireless telecommunications company, and NASCAR, the drive-fast-turn-left people, was announced Thursday. It means that as of 2004, the Winston Cup Series will become—take this slowly, now—the Nextel Cup Series.

This means more than a funny new name and new logos pasted on track billboards. It's the end of a more than 30-year relationship with the Winston cigarette brand. And, perhaps, another step in the de-Southernization of stock car racing.

Even aside from all the money and promises of increased media exposure, this is a big cultural shift. Consider the differences between these products. Cigarettes you can buy at the Pump 'n' Pay on your way to the races. Cell-phone contracts involve listening to salesmen expound on the wonders of Java-enabled wireless solutions on a packet-data network and methods for rounding off online minutes. It's moving from a product you could buy from a pull-knob vending machine next to the juke box at the back of a bar to a product that has the word "paradigm" in its sales pitches.

An end of an era.

This suggests a sponsor who is seeking a different sort of race fan than much of the crowd partying in the infield. With different—and more profitable—patterns of consumption. Fans who are more upscale, younger, shave on Saturdays, and seldom feel the need to tear the sleeves off their T-shirts.

This has been in the works for a long time. Last year, R. J. Reynolds Tobacco Company announced it and NASCAR were going their separate ways. It cited "changing business dynamics." Meaning that by law and court settlements, it could not overtly market cigarettes to young people.

And NASCAR was getting uncomfortable with the limitations and criticism that go with promoting carcinogens.

Back in 1971, when the Winston Cup Series was the Grand National Series, that didn't worry anybody. Hey, a dangerous habit increasingly rejected by mainstream society paying for a dangerous sport mainstream society doesn't understand? A perfect fit.

Those days are long gone.

Will people get used to the new name? Sure, but some will take longer than others. Personally, I still call the race run close to the Fourth of July the Firecracker 400, but I'm in an aging minority there.

Besides, NASCAR fans tend to take advertising more in stride than other sport fans. Racing fans have always accepted that race cars are pretty much billboards that happen to go 180 mph. They get startled by flat surfaces without logos. Let baseball fans have tedious debates about the purity of the sport.

I suspect the name will get softened as people say it and make the phrase their own. The NesTale Cup. The NegsTale Cup. The Negstle Cup. The Folks Who Make Those Teeny Little Phones Cup . . .

I'll be listening. The nation is getting a lot more like the South, and the South—and NASCAR—is getting more like the rest of the country. Sometimes, though, the transition can be a mouthful.

June 2003

Postscript: The Nextel Cup becomes the Sprint Cup in 2008.

Politicians seeking NASCAR dads

When political consultants come up with new demographic categories that are supposed to make or break elections, I sometimes imagine them as action figures. Each in vacuum-packed clear plastic with their tiny little accessories scattered about them on their cardboard display card.

There was the soccer mom with cell phone, water bottle, bench cushion, and clipboard. There was the angry white male with AM radio, National Rifle Association card, and pack of smokes. There was the waitress mom with apron, order pad, and minimum-wage law notice like the one posted by the back door. There was the wired worker with handheld computer, Wi-Fi laptop, and venti mocha cappuccino. And now the NASCAR dad has been added to the series with his numbered cap, cooler, and Big Gulp.

Collect the series!

The NASCAR dad label is supposed to characterize rural and suburban, white, married working stiffs who make up most of the infield crowd at races. The exact details change according to who is explaining them. Classifications like this may be based on polling data, but there is both art and science at work here.

As a person who lives in the capital of the NASCAR dad universe, I think it's easy to detect the faint aroma of condescension in the term. It might exist because people are too polite to talk about the Bubba vote anymore. Or maybe it's a way of widening the Bubba vote beyond the borders of the former Southern breakaway republic while cleaning him up, marrying him off to Lou-Anne, and making him more upscale.

Regardless of their precise identity, NASCAR dads tended to vote for George W. Bush in 2000. Democratic poll-readers say the party needs to win them back. They characterize them as swing-voters and ticket-splitters more loyal to their racing teams than to political parties. And therefore still ripe for the picking.

The term began appearing last summer, and now that the political season is warming up, I'm noticing it with increasing frequency.

A milestone in the NASCAR dad label arrived on the Fourth of July holiday when Florida's Senator Bob Graham took the designation literally and sponsored a truck in the 250-mile NASCAR Craftsman Truck Series race in Kansas. The truck, Number 50, driven by Jon Wood, won with

Graham's name displayed prominently in extra-bold, sans serif letters across the side of the bed.

From an advertising perspective, this was considered a novel move and something of a risk. For if Wood had finished at the back of the pack, you could guess what headline writers and wise-guy newspaper columnists would have done with that. The Graham campaign was already fighting the perception that it wasn't exactly in the passing lane.

But I applaud the move. I'd rather see campaign dollars go to racing trucks than to darkening the TV screens with negative advertising. Any presidential campaign that has a racing team, Jimmy Buffett, and a salsa campaign song ("Arriba Bob!") is moving American politics in a better direction.

The last time I wrote about NASCAR dads, I received an outraged e-mail from a Hispanic NASCAR fan who said I didn't appreciate the diversity of racing's fan-base. Well, yes, a lot of Hispanics go to the races. But even though he's a dad who is into NASCAR, he cannot, in the pollster sense of the term, be a NASCAR dad. Particularly since he lives in a city.

I just report the pollster constructs, sir, I don't make them up. And as a former soccer dad, I sympathize. Neither of us is supposed to exist.

September 2003

5 Symbolic politics

"When setting to work on a ballot, a Florida voter just sees more possibilities than other people—and is that so bad?"

—*The Darwinian Gardener's Almanac*

Illustration by Bruce Beattie.

Interview: Tallahassee Insider

I am sitting behind a beaded curtain in a discreet, out-of-the-way booth in a Tallahassee restaurant. It's an older place that still serves prime rib in portions as big as your head. The walls are decorated with framed black-and-white glossies of movers and shakers who, sadly, no longer move or shake.

I am here to speak with one of the most-quoted people every legislative session. None other than the Tallahassee Insider.

You've seen the name in all the papers—"'This group is going to be in session until Halloween,' a Tallahassee insider said recently." Or: "Tallahassee insiders were not surprised at the legislative logjam."

To conjure him, sidle into an inconspicuously located booth and have the waitress place an order of prime rib on the empty side of the table. You make sure the lights are dim. Then you recite, "Oh, insider who walks among us, feed yourself and feed me self-serving quotes! Tallahassee Insider. Tallahassee Insider. Tallahassee Insider!"

The magic works. As it usually does. I catch a faint whiff of sulfur and see his shadowy outline.

"Whatcha say?" I ask, flipping open my notebook and trying to sound nonchalant.

"I shouldn't even be talking to you," he snaps at me. "You quoted Capitol Insider in that last piece. That guy frosts my shorts."

"It wasn't me. It was an editor. He changed the wording. He thought you two were the same person."

"Happens way too often," the form sighs.

"But listen. You told me this session would last . . . oh, what was it . . . 'until the middle of shark-attack season.' But look around. Everyone went home."

"Oh, come on, they'll be back Tuesday. Not even I was cynical enough to think they'd declare victory and adjourn without passing a budget or doing that reorganization thing that the big ol' constitution of ours says they gotta do. Did you catch the bit with poppin' the champagne and the group hugs? I was afraid they were going to start joining hands and singing *Kumbaya*. It gets more embarrassing around here every year."

"So what now?"

"Here's what you can say. 'Tallahassee insiders could not remember the last time the legislature adjourned without passing a budget.'"

"I knew you wouldn't let me down."

"That's what I'm here for."

"But it's still going to be one dull special session this week," I complain. "They won't get to talk about anything except education reorganization. Where's the fun in that?"

"One Tallahassee insider said that you could define a ham sandwich as 'educational reorganization' if the speaker needs your vote."

"You're cooking tonight!" I exclaim, and I think I detect a smile.

"But what about a budget? They're going to have to have one eventually," I prod.

"Could be a train wreck, but calmer heads will prevail. It's the art of the possible. All it takes is a show of leadership. That's just how things work around here. We can't throw money at the problem. It's not over 'til the fat lady sings. Sooner or later, everyone's gotta put their cards on the table. And the clock is ticking. . . ."

He's fading into the booth's darkness already, and I'm writing as fast as I can. These are enough insights to last me for the next two months.

"Slow down!" I plead, but it's too late. There's only the faintest wisp of him left.

"The system works," the disembodied voice assures me.

Drat. Never enough time.

I look across the table, and I feel strangely encouraged. Maybe he's right. He always is in the end. And what's more, he hardly touched his steak fries.

March 2002

Prop: The plywood portable classroom

You can tell when an object has become a symbol of something: politicians start to visit it.

Portable classrooms are becoming symbolic, and sure enough, politicians are lining up to be near them.

Portable classrooms are symbolic of how crummy and overcrowded Florida schools are. Governor Lawton Chiles has been visiting them at a regular clip ever since the legislature let out. Jeb Bush, who has all but measured the governor's office for nicer drapes, is not to be outdone. He, too, is looking at portable classrooms and shaking his head at them at a respectable rate.

Shaking your head at a beat-up, 20-year-old portable shows you care. If anyone doubts you care, I suggest you try it. There are 17,000 portables in Florida. Plenty for everyone who needs to have their picture taken with one.

Portables are odd objects for so much attention. They are boxy, made mostly of plywood, and are supposed to be a temporary fix for overcrowding. In practice, though, once you see one towed to the playing field of your child's elementary school, the outfield will be lost until the kid's in college.

As a product of the Florida public school system, I have many rich memories of portables:

—The way they sound when an errant kickball hits them square on the side. *POM!* Brick schools lack that kind of dramatic resonance. Even a well-placed impact on a main school building cannot make near the sound or make things fall off a wall.

—The way they can be converted into haunted houses for Halloween carnivals. Not very convincing outside, no matter how much black crepe paper you use, but inside, in the dark, you can do a lot. The hollow-sounding, sometimes uneven floors are a definite bonus. And the wind noises, too, if the weather is just right.

—The way the old ones smell after a few days of heavy rain. Smells from childhood can bring memories back in a rush. Mold always takes me back to school. A few days of rain and the carpet under the portable's windows and doors would stay damp for weeks after the sun came out.

—The way everyone looked after running out to the portable in a downpour. Even the girls who fiercely flaunted their faultless fluffy hair looked like recently revived drowning victims. The boys would shake themselves like dogs. My glasses would fog over with moisture, turning the whole scene into a haze.

—The day the file cabinet fell. Actually, it only sank a little on one side because the floor beneath it was starting to get squishy. The Leaning File Cabinet of English was something I'd stare at in class, hoping to see it lurch, then disappear through the floor as though sucked down a mine shaft. Never happened. But the possibility was a pleasure to contemplate.

—The kid who ran under the portable and wouldn't come out. Portables are up off the ground on concrete blocks. That leaves plenty of room underneath. Two elementary school teachers tried to talk the kid out and he wouldn't budge. I was shooed away before he emerged. I assume he did, but who knows? Local legend said he stayed there until summer.

—The way rain sounds on the roof. Regular school roofs are high up and well insulated, but in a portable it's like being in a cabin on a lake or in the bleacher seats under the ballpark's overhang. The rain pings and taps. It's a cozy feeling, isolated from the other classes. At least when you are not wondering if the wind might blow the thing over.

—The spot where the bad kid kicked in the wall. Troubled youth are not usually threats to architecture, but the plywood in portables is pretty thin. One errant demonstration of kung fu technique can create a lasting impression that kids will visit and talk about for the rest of the year. After a few weeks, everyone will forget it was a kick mark and claim the kid created this crater with his bare hands. No, with his head!

Sadly, these warm moments cannot be experienced during a quick photo-opportunity. Maybe if legislative office buildings were expanded by putting lawmakers in little plywood cabins in back of the Capitol, they would gain a better appreciation.

Just as a temporary measure, of course.

October 1997

Prop: Generic Senior

You don't know me, but I can tell by the look on your face you're trying to figure out why I seem so familiar. Maybe it's this gravelly, sincere voice. Maybe it's the look of helpless worry I do so well. Listen. Hear that slow, soft, tinkly piano solo that plays in the background when I appear. Figured it out yet?

Yup, I'm the Generic Senior. I've dominated your television screen all month. And just wait 'til this week is over. By the time the polls open, you're going to want to put me in the old- television-advertising-folks home.

At least you will if there's still a Medicare program around to pay for it by then. If I haven't lost my home to confiscatory property taxes by then. If they haven't taken away Social Security by then. If they haven't tossed me into the streets so they can pay for smaller class sizes by then.

You see, this is what I do best. Worry.

Yeah, yeah, I hear you. Old people worrying is a cultural stereotype. Well, let me reassure you: personally, I'm not worried. I have way more work than I can handle.

Every producer of political ads is calling my agent this year. We gotta have Generic Senior to look worried that he'll lose Social Security to Wall Street sharpies after it's privatized. We gotta have Generic Senior to bravely fight back tears at the prospect of going untreated because Congress can't get its act together on prescription drug coverage. We gotta have Generic Senior who needs tax relief or the bank will foreclose. We gotta have Generic Senior whose life will be destroyed by politicians cutting Medicare.

When I get this stricken, helpless look on my face, grown people cry. I know. I've sat with the focus groups. One time I had to personally convince this sobbing woman that I'm just an actor, and that the bureaucrats, lawyers, and career politicians weren't really going to turn off my oxygen tank. All the survey work had to come to a stop. It's only a campaign ad, lady! I feel great. Sheesh.

Last election cycle, I lost a lot of work to that snotty little Generic Schoolkid. Always waving his little hand in the air. Me, me, call on me! Annoying little squirt. He and his friends were everywhere with politicians standing in front of chalkboards.

There're fewer of them this year. Education is a touchier issue now, and people have figured out that happy little Generic Schoolkid doesn't vote. A demanding little know-it-all, if you ask me. And don't even get me started about that whiny Concerned Housewife. As I've told the ad guys before and I tell them now, I'm more versatile than either of them.

I can be in an attack ad and it won't feel like an attack ad. Republicans use me to attack Democrats and the class-size amendment. Democrats use me to attack Republicans who want to privatize Social Security.

And both parties need me to swell up with pride at the sight of Old Glory or cringe with fear at a future darkened by politicians, personal injury lawyers, greedy HMOs, career criminals walking the streets, or whoever else is doing mischief. Both parties need Generic Senior to melt with gratitude in front of Representative Incumbent who is looking out for me in Washington.

So don't hate me because you're sick of seeing my face in campaign ads every hour of every day. Yeah, I feel your pain, but I'm just doing my job. And as those baby boomers age, my agent won't be able to answer the phone fast enough. Which is why I don't care what the heck they do to Social Security. I'm not retiring any time soon.

Heh, heh, that's me, Generic Senior. And don't even think of attempting that warm chuckle, bucko. It's a registered trademark.

October 2002

Testimonial: AVC

You might wonder why I am not a communist. I do, after all, wear a beard and have beady, little piglike eyes. The answer is simple. I was saved by the Florida legislature.

That great bunch in Tallahassee required me by law to enroll in thirty hours of instruction in "Americanism versus Communism" if I aspired to become a high school graduate. The statute, as it currently reads, mandates instruction in "the dangers of communism, the ways to fight communism, the evils of communism, the fallacies of communism, and the false doctrines of communism."

Lest anyone fail to catch the general drift of the law, the state textbook council is required to select the texts for the course guided by "the official reports of the House Un-American Activities [Committee] and the Senate Internal Security Subcommittee of the United States Congress." A neat trick in 1989 since both have been out of existence for two decades.

But getting out of high school is a powerful motivator. And I would still be there today if I hadn't taken a seat in an auditorium with fifty other kids and listened to a full exposition on the dangers of communism, the ways to fight communism, the evils of communism, the fallacies of communism, and the false doctrines of communism.

The teacher was a small, thin woman who often had to shout to be heard in the back rows of the auditorium where the troublemakers sat. Where, for some reason, I sat, too. This had a way of making the presentation sound a little shrill.

In fairness, though, what she had to say was not entirely uninteresting to a 15-year-old since she often offered detailed accounts of the varied ways communists executed people. I can still hear the staccato phrases she shouted in between the parts I didn't quite catch.

"The whole family . . . even the dog . . . bodies dissolved in acid . . . Are you listening in back? There's going to be a quiz!"

By the time the school year was in its final stretch and the auditorium was getting warm, she found we had covered the dangers of communism, the ways to fight communism, the evils of communism, and the fallacies of communism but had slighted the false doctrines of communism. So she redoubled her efforts.

Almost every day the AV kids wheeled in a 16mm projector so we could

Orange grove American Party sign, West Volusia County. (Photo by Mark Lane)

see black-and-white films sponsored by the electric company about how communists were taking over the world and how the average citizen might respond.

I was convinced. The communists, I decided, must be very horrible people to subject me to hours of jumpy 16mm films shown in a hot, dark room with an otherwise nice lady shouting at me about dissolving bodies in acid.

Somewhere in the Volusia County School System's records' basement is a typewritten form. One line says "Lane, Mark: Americanism vs. Communism Grade: B, Conduct U." "U" stood for "unsatisfactory." Not a shining moment in my academic career. If communists had taught the course they would have dissolved my body in acid.

Still, I passed. And I'm still not a communist. The course must have done its job. It worked so well, it made me dislike propaganda of any kind. Even the kind my government produces.

Now, when I hear a philosophy that has the future figured out a little too neatly, I imagine its precepts shouted by a woman in a hot auditorium to bored and uncomprehending teens. I hear it on the wavering soundtrack of a 16mm film. Few theories of government, history, and the universe sound very grand after that.

I'd like to think that's the kind of skepticism the legislature was trying to inculcate. But somehow, I'm just not so sure.

November 1989

Postscript: The American Versus Communism statute was repealed by the legislature in 1989. I shaved my beard about the same time.

Election 2000: Irregularities

It's all very flattering to know our votes count extra hard in Florida. But if I had my druthers, some other state would be the one to have the final say in this election.

It's not that we're the wrong people to dictate what's good for the rest of the country. We're qualified. It's just that when it comes to counting votes, well, we have something of a past. The English can't cook, Germans can't do comedy, and Floridians can't hold an untainted election. It's just a cultural thing.

Only three years ago, Miami's mayoral election was so breathtakingly fraudulent, even by South Florida standards, that the courts overturned it, and fifty-six people faced criminal charges. Four years ago in Volusia County, the absentee ballot handling was so irregular that a court had to declare the winner in the sheriff's race more than two months afterward. To this day, speculating on the identity of "the real sheriff" is a sure-fire way to start a fight in a crowded room.

And the last time the nation looked to Florida and Volusia County to decide the winner of a presidential race in which the popular vote and the electoral vote diverged? Oh, don't ask. It was bad. Very bad.

In 1876 Florida only had four electoral votes, but they were four electoral votes that mattered. With most of the nation's ballots counted, Democrat Samuel J. Tilden was ahead by a quarter-million votes and only one electoral vote short of victory. Republican Rutherford B. Hayes needed the electoral votes of Florida, Louisiana, and South Carolina to win.

About fifty thousand ballots were cast in Florida—the exact number will never be known—and Hayes and Tilden were less than one hundred votes apart.

Historians think Tilden probably won the state. Who knows? Ballot mishandling, fraud, selective vote counting, and intimidation were the rule, not the exception.

A true hometown election story: in New Britain, now Ormond Beach, the residents, mostly Republican New Englanders, voted overwhelmingly for Hayes. Loomis Day, the son of Daytona Beach founder Matthias Day, had a pretty good idea of how local politics worked and suspected that safe delivery of Republican ballots to the county seat in Enterprise would be no sure thing. (The county seat would be moved to DeLand a dozen years later after, yes, a disputed election.)

Day took the ballot box by wagon to Enterprise but had somebody else carry a fake ballot box to Enterprise by another road. Sure enough, the decoy ballot box was snatched en route. The real ballot box made it to town, and the votes were duly entered.

New Year's Day 1877 arrived without a winner. Pundits of the day speculated about another civil war. Rioting in the streets was expected. Congress received three different sets of results from Florida. The first canvassing board declared the state for Hayes, a rival board declared it for Tilden, and in January 1877, a third board appointed by the new governor certified the election for Tilden.

Ultimately, Congress's Electoral Commission awarded Florida's electoral votes to Hayes. The decision was the culmination of a deal that ended Reconstruction, prevented renewed regional conflict, and sold out the basic rights of Southern black people for generations.

Given this overly rich history, you really don't want to depend on Florida elections to pick the Leader of the World's Greatest Superpower. I'm not sure I would want Florida's election system to pick the MTV Video Music Awards.

Meanwhile in Volusia County, the elections office is wrapped in yellow crime scene tape. There have been mysterious counting fluctuations, ballots found in the back seat of a poll worker's car, and registered voters turned away at the polls. There were lost ballots in South Florida. And in Palm Beach, they had a ballot laid out with the clarity of a VCR programming diagram.

The tradition lives on.

November 2000

Election 2000: Hand count in DeLand

A woman in large, red-framed glasses flips up a ballot so it faces the woman across the table. "Bush," the woman says. Another flips. "Gore." It looks like a political Rorschach test is in progress or a fast and partisan eye exam. The women seated on either side of the ballot reader nod in unison.

Bush, Bush, Bush, Gore . . .

The rhythm doesn't flag, each ballot is sorted and stacked within ten seconds. It's Monday afternoon and about thirty such teams are doing the same thing in a first-floor training room in the Thomas C. Kelly Administration Center, DeLand.

Gore, Bush, Gore, Gore . . .

The soft murmur of the presidential candidates' names fills the room like monks' chanting.

Bush, Gore, Bush, Gore . . .

"Hold on, the bubble isn't filled in all the way," a Republican observer objects. The Democrat frowns but says nothing. The ballot goes in the disputed pile. Disputed ballots are put in large manila envelopes and sent to the canvassing board's table.

The creativity with which Volusia County voters attack a ballot is something to behold. "Completely fill in the oval next to your choice as shown," say the instructions at the top of each ballot. Yet voters check the lozenge-shaped ovals. They X them. They slash them. They demurely dot them. Sometimes they ignore the ovals entirely and put checks and Xs next to the names of their candidates. Sometimes they enthusiastically fill in the oval next to their candidate's name and write out the name on the write-in line in large block letters for extra good measure. Sometimes they carefully fill in one oval then write Xs over a second name.

The envelopes of questionable ballots are brought to the canvassing board's pile in a far corner of the room. Each is opened by County Judge Michael McDermott. He holds it up. A motion is made as to how it should count. It is seconded and voted on, then the next ballot goes up.

The process usually takes under thirty seconds. A stenographer records the discussion. A Republican observer snaps photos of disputed ballots with a digital camera.

Most of these ballots do not require much of a judgment call. There are partial fill-ins, sloppy fill-ins that explode from the lines, Xs in circles, and checks by names. Each is obvious to a human eye. Most are unintelligible to an automated counter.

"Cast ballot for Al Gore," says County Council member Ann McFall regarding a ballot with a checked oval.

"Second," says County Council member Pat Northey in a beat.

"Opposed?" asks McDermott. A two-second pause. "Ballot cast for Al Gore."

A new ballot is flipped. This is repeated for over forty hours.

Gore, Bush, Bush, Bush . . .

"This is surreal," says Northey during a rare break. In the roped-off area, Republican observers talk into cell phones, television cameramen position themselves for a new angle, reporters wander by, and sheriff's deputies stand watchfully. News organizations from as far away as Tokyo are set up in a big white media tent.

Northey says that in the weekend of canvassing no more than a half-dozen ballots have been matters of serious debate.

To keep things moving, the event is catered by the county Department of Corrections. Jail food. "We had barbecue pork today," she says cheerily as she rejoins the board. "With coleslaw."

Gore, Bush, Gore, Gore . . .

Outside, a handful of Republican protesters stand with signs on the old courthouse's steps across from the line of television trucks, their antennae bristling like a wharf full of sailboats. A middle-aged woman stands at stiff attention with both hands grasping an elaborate large sign bedecked with American and Florida flags. "Stop counting!!! Man Voted. Machine counted. Now Man Manipulates. GOD SAVE THE USA!" it shouts.

Bush, Bush, Gore, Gore . . .

Inside the count is winding down, and the chanting of candidates' names softens as teams finish their work and drift away, leaving the canvassing board to work until around 11 p.m.

Tuesday, work resumes at 8 a.m. This time the counting comes down to one table, the canvassing board and a single stack of ballots in red envelopes in a plastic bin. These are problem ballots. Ballots that could not be counted at the precincts and had been stored in the "emergency bin," a locked drawer on the left side of a vote-tabulating machine. There are more than one hundred of them. Republican attorneys object to their inclusion. "The chain of ballot custody cannot be determined," they argue.

The debate is cut short with news that the state Department of Elections deadline for certified totals will not be waived.

"We have been informed that the judge in Tallahassee has denied our motion," announces McDermott.

It is 1 p.m. This means the count must be complete and certified by 5 p.m. The work becomes a race against the clock. Throughout the afternoon, three women click furiously at adding machines in the back of the room. The board, meanwhile, proceeds with the emergency-bin ballots.

"Cast ballot for George Bush."

"Second."

"Opposed? . . . Ballot cast for George Bush."

This is repeated 115 times.

Volusia County's long count was completed only five minutes before the deadline and handed off to a courier from the Department of Elections. Gore, 97,304 Volusia County votes; Bush, 82,357. Gore gained 98 votes from the original count. This closed a remarkable push to redeem Volusia County's flawed election-day performance. That the canvassing board, elections office, and county pulled off the hand-counting of more than 184,000 ballots in four days is nothing short of amazing.

The closeness of this race cast a harsh spotlight on every phase of balloting in Florida and Volusia County. The voters who marked ballots in goofy ways. The tabulation system that malfunctioned, losing and misreporting vote totals. The poll workers who misplaced ballots, delivered them late, turned voters away, and improvised when things went wrong. The kind of glitches common in local elections now is affecting the nation's choice for president.

What followed was an all-out effort to restore the legitimacy of Volusia's vote count. More than three hundred people participated in the counting. Some worked in more than twelve-hour shifts for three days, battling fatigue, dealing with mind-numbing detail, and handling partisan disputes dispassionately, even gracefully. It was paper-sorting as an Olympic event, a ballot-counting bee. And all completed under the glare of television lights and the eyes of people with stakes in the outcome.

What happens next will be up to the lawyers, the candidates, Congress, and the courts. Whatever the decision, nobody can argue that Volusia County didn't take heroic measures to make sure its voters were heard and heard right.

November 2000

Letter: Bob Graham

Dear Senator Graham,

I hope you received the $5 I mailed for political buttons before you went on *Larry King Live*. Too bad the Siegfried and Roy segment ate up most of the show. I guess being mauled by a real-live tiger is always more newsworthy than being mauled by the political process. I guess people like their news to be literal rather than metaphorical.

Anyway, I sent in the order so I'd have one button for myself and four to sell on eBay. I saw a 1984 Reubin Askew for President button there a few months back for $12 (plus shipping). No kidding.

The political button collectable market is a funny thing, Senator Graham. It does not reward success. A winning presidential contender will scatter buttons around the country for more than a year. It saturates the market.

I have this Clinton-Gore button the size of Wayne Newton's belt buckle and saw one just like it on eBay for $1.75, without one bid. George W. Bush buttons sell by the pound.

People have this way of hanging on to a winner's campaign material and tossing the loser's. It's a kind of denial. Just look at bumper stickers. People will drive around for years with a winning bumper sticker on their car, but the defeated scrape stickers off their cars by the light of a flashlight while you can still hear the voices of experts parsing exit-poll results on television.

But I digress.

Smart guy that you are, you have probably guessed that the order—did I say $5? enclosed is $3 more to bring it to $8—was not a vote of confidence. After your aides and consultants began bailing last month, I figured the show was closing.

Which is a shame, but not your fault. I guess Florida politicians just don't export so well. Look at poor Askew. He was one of the state's really great governors, but he lacked the charisma, charm, and vote-getting appeal of Walter Mondale. Which I suppose is saying something.

Florida is a big state now. This is a truth that a lot us who grew up here are still getting used to. We're so big that anyone who becomes governor immediately starts considering whether he wants to be president or vice president. It's been like that since Claude Kirk. (Just try finding *his* buttons. Both parties united in expunging all traces of the man.)

Strange how the things that made you popular in Florida—a low-key style, the tendency to break into song at odd moments, the undisguised quirkiness, cool campaign ideas like sponsoring a NASCAR truck, the stances that didn't fit into a fixed ideology, the maroon tie with little white Florida outlines—were the very things that flummoxed the out-of-state media.

The bit about writing every little thing into color-coded notebooks so baffled the news guys that they couldn't focus on anything else. Won't it be nice to be able to go back to doing that out in the open again?

But hey, at least you didn't have to be eaten by wild animals to get on *Larry King Live*, right?

Hope you're not too disappointed and will come home soon. And don't bother sending a Graham for Senate button. I've got plenty of those, and for the reasons stated above, they aren't worth much.

Make that another $2 to bring the order to $10. Remember: presidential pins only.

Thank you in advance.

P.S. After filling my order, it would be a very good idea to destroy the remaining buttons. Knowing you have a few boxes ready to go would only create a temptation in the future, and all those buttons have the potential for really depressing the market for years to come. Best to destroy them fast.

October 2003

Buzz phrase: Smart growth

The people I'll vote for in the county council races are all for smart growth. So are the people my neighbors will vote for. I bet your guy is, too. That's because this year just about everyone in fast-growing parts of the county is foursquare for smart growth.

And, yes, I don't know what they mean by the phrase either. But how can you disagree with someone who says we should try to act smart when it comes to growth? No one can say Florida hasn't tried the alternative.

All city and county elections across Florida revolve around some form of land-use policy—at least when they don't revolve around criminal records. Sometimes the immediate issues are overcrowded roads and schools. Sometimes the issue is sprawl eating up scenic byways and wildlife habitat. Sometimes the issues are fire and ambulance services that are overextended to cover new parts of town. Sometimes it's taxes being increased to build schools and stretch city services for new subdivisions. Sometimes it has to do with still having drinking water in a few years. But all these things come down to what gets built where.

The choice, if the campaign literature is to be believed, is between fast-growth types, people who say the future will take care of itself and pay for itself, and no-growth types, people who think they can create islands of fixed population in a state whose laws and economy are geared to inviting everyone to come on down. Or, put more pungently, between land-rapists and tree-huggers.

You cannot win public office as a land-rapist. You cannot win public office as a tree-hugger. This usually leaves candidates advocating moderate growth. A choice between land-harassers and tree-patters.

This, too, is unsatisfying. Moderate growth can turn into runaway growth with two or three rezonings. And it often does. Long-term, we-really-mean-it master plans have a way of changing anytime two guys wearing suits show up at a publicly owned microphone with a PowerPoint presentation.

Since no candidate wants to be a land-rapist or tree-hugger, and since nobody believes anyone who talks about moderate growth, a new label is needed and needed desperately. That label is *smart growth*.

Like most buzz phrases, this actually did have a meaning before it became popular. An outgrowth of the new urbanism planning philosophies that emerged in the 1990s, smart growth usually means striving toward development that de-emphasizes cars, encourages mixed land uses within a development, tries to maximize open spaces, and strives to build in ways that encourage community. It smiles on building closer to a town center rather than ever farther outward. It encourages having businesses close to homes to take pressure off roads.

In practice, though, it often means putting up a gas station and strip mall near the entrance to a new development at the edge of town and being sure to have landscaping with trees, sidewalks, and maybe a bike path next to the sales office. A few white picket fences, too, since they practically guarantee a sense of community.

When used in political forums, though, the term *smart growth* usually means what *moderate growth* or *growth management* used to mean. It's a way of saying, "Okay, we won't approve battery recycling plants, toxic waste dumps, more mobile home parks, or anything bad and ugly unless the lawyers say we have to." Which, I suppose, is progress of a sort.

So next time you're at a candidate forum, be sure to ask the candidates just what they mean when they talk about this thing they call smart growth. But only do that if it's not already late in the evening. The results can be pretty time-consuming.

August 2004

For: The Florida Residency Certificate Plan

Just so we're all clear, a newspaper column isn't really a newspaper column unless it is a mix of what we laughingly call reality along with assertions that fall within the more airy confines of opinion.

Readers who write to complain that something in a column is nothing more than an opinion are out of sympathy not only with the writer but with the writer's whole line of work. Like people who criticize rock lyrics for not making sense, they just don't get the act.

I have received a lot of criticism in this vein from people who object to things I've written about growth and civic planning in Florida. People tell me that when characterizing sprawl as a Bad Thing, I am doing no more than grunting a personal opinion. True enough. I am advancing just another unrealistic and subjective personal preference, which is what I do.

The second most common thing unhappy readers say is that by criticizing the fast-growth policies traditional in Florida cities, I want to slam the door shut behind me. To which I also have a ready response: "Darn tootin'." I would *love* to slam the door shut behind me.

Of course, I arrived in 1962 as a little kid and would not advocate capping Florida's population at Kennedy-era levels. That would be extreme. I'm a reasonable guy. I'd be willing to go up to, say, 1980.

What's more, I can even imagine a way to shut the door behind me. And it would have significant advantages to everybody around me. It would separate people who really want to live here from the half-hearted. It would put cash in the pockets of regular people and would be a source of revenue for the state.

Yes, it has a few minor drawbacks. One is that it would be howlingly unconstitutional. But advocating things that are howlingly unconstitutional and daring the courts to say anything happens to be in style just now. Regardless, here's the plan:

Everybody now in Florida can stick around. Fair's fair. But nobody else can move in until somebody else moves out. One U-Haul trailer in, one U-Haul trailer out. Now, Florida is an appealing place, and some people will still want to move here. In fact, knowing there will be less population pressure would make people want to come here all the more. That's okay.

It's okay because some people who moved here didn't do their homework. They are surprised at how hot August gets. They complain that nobody who lives within sight of a beach has a work ethic. They don't like going to places where you order lunch in Spanish. The wildlife, lightning, hurricanes, and giant bugs scare them. The humidity oppresses them.

People like these could put their Florida Resident Certificates for sale on eBay. Maybe they'd sell them to a residential permit broker. The market would work out the details. People who want to move here would buy the certificates, and sellers would have thirty days to clear out. I bet the proceeds would more than pay for the moving van.

The state would get, say, 10 percent on the sale to pay for any new services the newcomers might demand. Newcomers have a way of demanding things.

Because state residency would now be worth a dollar figure, people would value living here more. They'd take more pride in the place. They'd take more of an interest in what the legislature and county commissions are doing to the value of their certificates. What's more, the market price of a certificate would be an excellent gauge of the quality of life around here.

It is, as they say in the movies, just crazy enough to work. But that's just an opinion.

September 2006

For: Our national registered trademark

I rise to speak in favor of the flag bill. No, not the Flag Desecration Constitutional Amendment. That one went down by one vote last week. I speak instead about a Flag Copyright Act.

Lately, we've been hard at work in this chamber passing every new copyright crackdown that our friends and contributors in the information and entertainment industries can cook up. It's a global information economy out there, folks, and we can't have people grabbing data, symbols, and works of art for free anytime they feel like it.

So I was coming out of the committee room after hearing more Hollywood and music industry attorneys telling us how everybody's going broke and they need more legal tools for going after people downloading and using their products, when suddenly something occurred to me.

What is our nation's flag but a symbol, work of art, and trademark for the greatest nation on the whole wired planet? And we're treating it like it's an open-source commodity. Something anyone can use for free, monkey around with, adapt to their products, use for promotional and decorative purposes—use however they want, whenever they want.

Well, ladies and gentlemen, this nation was not founded on the proposition that people get to use stuff for free. Yet here is our national emblem being used copyright-free, on a do-it-yourself, giveaway basis.

What gives, people?

Under a Flag Copyright Act, the U.S. government would own the copyright to the American flag. If you want to burn the flag—diminishing the value of our national copyrighted trademark—our lawyers just might need to have a sit-down talk with you within twenty days of receiving a summons. If you create a goofy piece of art riffing off our copyrighted national trademark, Uncle Sam might want a piece of its astounding asking price.

We are running a federal budget deficit of close to $300 billion. The Iraq war alone is costing $6 billion a month. This nation needs some new income without taxing our celebrated entrepreneurial spirit. And what better way to do that than for the nation to get a cut anytime somebody uses Old Glory for crass commercial purposes?

Giant flags over car dealerships that help draw customers? We'd ask for no more than pennies per vehicle. Lee Greenwood CDs? He would be proud to give America its cut of the royalties. Flag-draped, mass-mailed fundraising appeals done in the name of the red, white, and blue? We ask no more than the American people's share.

I and everyone else in public office have to wear these little American flag lapel pins all the time. What if the government got a nickel a pin? I'll tell you what: no more scrounging around for extra Humvee armor.

Better still, this might prevent, or at least cut down on, uses of the flag that fall short of desecration but still hack off many right-thinking Americans. Like those American-flag thong bathing suits. Sad to say, many women who wear them simply do not have a realistic body-image.

And here's the beauty part: to accomplish this, we wouldn't have to open the hood on the U.S. Constitution and start messing around with the wiring. A simple law would do it.

We'd unleash the lawyers on all four or five flag burners who surface each year. We'd raise money for the war. And we'd send a message about how wrong it is to let people use symbols and works of art, gratis, for no money at all. Everybody's a winner.

I yield the remainder of my time.

June 2006

Against: Florida license plates

My complaints about the standard-issue Florida license plate have been a matter of public record for years. Specifically, the undisputed fact that the fruit illustrated on the plate does not resemble anything found in nature. It has the leaves of a peach and the smooth texture of a peach, yet the shape and color of an orange. The more you stare at one of these things—and this is Florida, so one spends a fair amount of time parked on the road behind cars bearing this tag—the odder it looks. I keep looking for the slogan, "Florida salutes genetically modified foods!"

It is gratifying, then, to hear that the governor and cabinet are aware of this problem and propose doing something about it when the tag's five-year expiration date rolls around in October.

"If you like the orange, you're going to have to defend it," Governor Jeb Bush warned Fred Dickinson, director of the Department of Highway Safety and Motor Vehicles, at a Cabinet meeting Tuesday.

But rather than send the DMV folks back to the office to look for somebody who could draw an orange, the cabinet members advanced all kinds of ideas. Hold a contest, they said. Let little kids design it, they said. Make it match the state coin. Put a space shuttle, a galleon, Cypress Garden skiers, and a shining sun with sunglasses on it. Okay, the last couple were my ideas, but firmly in the spirit of things.

Politicians are by nature unable to come up with even mediocre graphic statements. For proof, look at the state symbols on the backs of U.S. quarters. Some of them are so stuffed with baffling state iconography that they look like little "Where's Waldo?" puzzles. Similarly, Florida's symbol-packed state seal looks like a plate of scrambled eggs and bacon when the state flag is viewed from a distance.

Something about the political process lends itself to graphic piling-on. Get a legislative committee into the act and it will heap all kinds of things on our plate—a space shuttle, a galleon, a shining sun, Cypress Garden skiers, a heron, a gator, a proud Seminole, a leaping marlin, Jeb Bush holding an American flag and a BlackBerry, a steaming cup of Cuban coffee, In God We Trust, In Associated Industries of Florida We Trust, Mickey Mouse, Donald Duck, Andrew Jackson, and the Battle of Olustee. Just for starters.

Personally, I miss the Spartan simplicity of the state's pre-1978, stamped-out-by-prisoners-style plates. Big rounded letters and numbers, "Sunshine State" on the bottom, and that's that. No pictures. No graphic statements.

Instead, its minimalism was itself a message. And the message was "This is a car. I paid the state of Florida so I could drive it around another year. Beats walking. Beats living in New Jersey." Sentiments that unite us all.

Now, thanks to an overenthusiastic legislature, there is little unity on Florida roads. The highway is just one more place where Floridians have little in common with each other. We have more than fifty specialty tags of varying degrees of awfulness, and more are in the works.

Last week, Senator Steven Geller, D-Hallandale Beach, introduced the

"Design Your Own License Plate Act." It would allow anyone who gave $100 to a charity to get a blank auto tag complete with markers—permanent or wash-off—so they could draw a custom plate. Finally, the dream of a specialty tag for every Floridian would be within reach.

Under questioning, however, the senator admitted his amendment was only a little joke lampooning the endless number of new tags. Too bad. I like the idea. The cabinet and plate-design team should take note.

April 2003

Postscript: The new plate adopted by the state sported a more orangelike orange, the outline of the state, and the state government Web address. There are now 104 specialty plates with more in the works.

✳ ✳ ✳ ✳ ✳ ✳ ✳ ✳ ✳ ✳ ✳ ✳ ✳ ✳ ✳ ✳ ✳ ✳

For: Truth, Beauty, Decency, Cute Little Children, and Free Beer for Everyone (with Proper ID) Act

I rise to urge passage of the Truth, Beauty, Decency, Cute Little Children, and Free Beer for Everyone (with Proper ID) Act of 2004. The Truth, Beauty, Decency, Cute Little Children, and Free Beer for Everyone (with Proper ID) Act of 2004 is the natural successor to the Freedom, Motherhood, American Excellence, and All-You-Can-Eat Barbecue Act of 2003. It also incorporates a few elements of the Truth, Justice, and the American Way Act of 2001.

But do not worry. It does not contain the controversial sections of the Truth, Justice, and the American Way Act. The parts I'm sure you've already heard about from your constituents. Those provisions have been split off into the Hot Dogs in Summer, Daisies, and Smiles From Pretty Girls Act of 2004, which I hope you will also take time to consider.

The press has been unfair to the Truth, Beauty, Decency, Cute Little

Children, and Free Beer for Everyone (with Proper ID) Act. They compare it to the controversy over the Raindrops on Roses and Whiskers on Kittens Act of 2002.

The RRWKA, as you recall, sought merely to require computer manufacturers to install simple remote-controlled devices. That way the FBI could, without leaving the office, blow up any computer suspected of being used for terrorism or downloading Metallica songs.

Like you, I thought it would be enough to say, "Hey, how can I vote against the Raindrops on Roses and Whiskers on Kittens Act? I'd look like a monster." But that's just not good enough for some people. The overreaction by a misinformed public was the worst thing this congressman had seen since the Cream-Colored Ponies and Crisp Apple Strudel Act of 2000, which, it should be recalled, sought only to regulate the use of seersucker, not ban it altogether.

The rise of the Internet means our constituents get vicious misinformation and outright lies about legislation before we can even read a bill. It gets worse every session. I remind this chamber that the Girls in White Dresses with Blue Satin Sashes Act would have controlled this by having Internet users sign a simple loyalty oath and be liable for fines up to $500,000 for disseminating misinformation about pending legislation.

Some have ridiculed the Truth, Beauty, Decency, Cute Little Children, and Free Beer for Everyone (with Proper ID) Act for having nothing to do with truth, beauty, decency, cute little children, or free beer for everyone (with proper ID). Such criticism is so ignorant I don't know where to begin. Some people refuse to understand the democratic process.

What about the Little Green Apples Act of 1998? That imposed federal criminal penalties for vandalizing gumball machines. Or the Freedom for Children to be Free Act, which concerned food labeling, pinwheel safety standards, and the death penalty? Or the America is Number One and Don't You Forget It Act, which would have allowed sales of bazookas in flea markets?

This is just how we do things, people! Does nobody take basic civics courses anymore? (Courses, I might add, that would be mandatory under the Doorbells and Sleigh Bells and Schnitzel with Noodles Act of 2004.)

What about the USA PATRIOT Act? What about No Child Left Behind? The Defense of Marriage Act? Do any of these things have to with patriotism, leaving kids unattended, or keeping people married? Sheesh, it's like we have to explain the smallest thing.

I blame the public school system.

So I ask you to vote for the Truth, Beauty, Decency, Cute Little Children, and Free Beer for Everyone (with Proper ID) Act. It's a great improvement over its old draft, which was called the Neighborhood Toxic Waste Disposal Act. Or something like that.

April 2004

For: State bird reform

Not everyone shares my enthusiasm for the Florida legislature. But I look on the first Tuesday after the first Monday of March as something of a holiday. It kicks off a two-month period when the state's editorial writers and columnists may open their newspapers each morning confident that easy outrage and cheap comedy will leap from the pages. You just need to write it down fast enough.

This session should be no exception. Perusing the list of pre-filed bills one finds all the perennials.

Bills to gut the growth management law? Check. Bills to allow more secrecy at all levels of government? Check. Bills to create tax breaks for select little niches of commercial endeavor? Check, check, and the check is in the mail. Bills that are entirely symbolic yet still guaranteed to start an argument? Check.

I was particularly happy to find the return of some legislation in that last category: a bill to give Florida a better state bird.

I have long been a student of my state's weird array of official symbols. State statutes describe the official state soil as Myakka fine sand (and a fine sand it is). Our official state reptile may be bought in rubber replica at any better souvenir store. We have an official beverage, official butterfly, official fish (freshwater and saltwater), official flower, official wildflower, official gem, official shell, official stone, official tree, and official water mammal, both freshwater and saltwater.

Florida doesn't have a very strong identity. Even more than most states, we are still deciding who we are. This makes the quest for new symbols poignant, strange, and sometimes surprisingly heated. That happened last year when changing the official state bird was debated hotly.

The state bird currently is the mockingbird, a common, noisy, aggressive creature found everywhere in the continental United States. It's a bland state symbol that implies we don't have anything more interesting on the wing around here. The suggested replacement was the scrub jay, a bird found only in Florida but sadly in short supply.

But it was the bird's threatened status that got the attention of development interests who saw state bird designation as a propaganda tool for environmentalists. They imagined headlines like "Strip mall slated in state bird's habitat." Yet the development issue stayed strictly in the background during debate. Instead, opponents went negative on the scrub jay.

"They eat the eggs of other birds," huffed Marion Hammer, the veteran National Rifle Association lobbyist enlisted to fight the scrub jay menace. "That's criminal conduct, that's robbery and murder." She described the bird as "lazy," displaying "a welfare mentality." She almost called it a liberal.

With legislators deadlocked on which was the nicer bird, the bill died. Well, now the scrub jay bill is back for another try. This time, it says right in the legislation that "the designation of the Florida scrub jay is the official state bird is strictly symbolic and does not require any additional protections or acquisition of habitat."

There it is in black and white: just because it's the state bird doesn't mean we have to stop killing it. With this actually spelled out in the act, there should be no reason to oppose the little scrub jay.

Personally, I'd feel better with a limpkin or great white heron, but a scrub jay works fine for me. It's a native bird, and one that, like much of natural Florida, is every year steadily disappearing.

The legislators should assent and move to more pressing concerns. Like finding a hotter official state band or proudly designating key lime as the official state pie.

March 2000

Postscript: The second scrub jay bill died, too. And the friendly little bird's moral character was again attacked by indignant legislators and lobbyists.

For: State pie

The debate over the statutory status of Florida's state pie seems to be over before it began. Representative Dwight Stansel, D-Live Oak, told the *Miami Herald* last week that he was just kidding in his opposition to the measure. (Actually, "just cuttin' the fool" was the story's money quote.)

A pecan grower, Stansel has a special stake in this issue. Past attempts to honor key lime pie had come up against the hard-shell political power wielded by North Florida legislators on behalf of pecan pie.

Pecans grown commercially in Florida tend be grown near the Interstate-10 belt. And that was where the balance of power used to be not so very long ago.

Even as late as 1994, when then–state Representative Debbie Wasserman Schultz sponsored a similar measure in the Florida House, she had to settle for half a slice. A resolution declared key lime pie to be merely an "important symbol of Florida." Big whup.

Similar clashes of special interests had delayed honoring the orange as the official state fruit until only last year. Grapefruit growers had previously felt slighted by attempts to do this.

I have long been a student of the state's pantheon of official symbols. I like to think this column was at least partly responsible in 2004 for alerting an uncomprehending Senate to a backdoor attempt to supplant the state stone (the noble agatized coral) with a separate state rock (Ocala limestone) and state fossil (the Eocene heart urchin).

And I wasn't afraid to be in the forefront of doomed attempts to replace the state song ("Old Folks at Home" or "Suwannee River" or "Swanee Ribber") with something a bit less mournful, that smells less of burnt cork and doesn't need to have the word "darkeys" scrubbed from the lyrics when you force schoolchildren to sing it.

I was looking forward, then, to a good, old-fashioned pie fight. One that would pit North Florida against South Florida. Interstate 10 against State Road A1A. Calhoun County against Broward County. Nuts against fruits. Earth tones against pastels.

State pie status for key lime could be an excellent symbol of the half-century shift in state power from the rural, north, and western to the urban, south, and coastal. And it would be about time.

Not only is key lime pie less filling than pecan pie—which, let's face it, is far more associated with Georgia—but I like its symbolism. And that's what I look for in an official state food: taste and metaphor.

A key lime pie is a mix of the natural (eggs, limes) and the synthetic (cheap dye in the inauthentic versions, canned condensed milk in the authentic). Of the exotic and tropical (hard-to-find key limes) and the mundane (eggs, graham crackers.) Of the tart and the sweet. Of the cracker (graham) and the tropical (lime).

It can look garish when crassly made for the quick buck, or be bland on the outside yet sweetly rich within. A mix of opposites—and most of the ingredients come from somewhere else. What better state symbol can you find than that?

March 2006

Postscript: At press time, a bill to keep "Old Folks at Home" (with cleaned-up lyrics) as the state song and adopt "Where the Sawgrass Meets the Sky" as the new state anthem had passed committee votes but faced uncertain prospects before the full house and senate. One distinguished critic had described "Sawgrass" as sounding "like a mash-up of 'From a Distance,' 'O Canada,' and an infomercial from one of your slicker television ministries." Okay, I called it that. And I apologized to the people of Florida for encouraging an unequipped legislature to take up a matter this weighty.

For: Clear speaking

In his first executive order, Governor Charlie Crist told state officials to cut the gobbledygook and write clearly. Well, that's not exactly what the order said. What the order actually said was:

"Whereas, to further the goal of maximizing service by the public's servants, the people of Florida must have access to their state government and their elected and appointed officials, our state government must be responsive to citizens who seek assistance from it, and our state government must communicate in a clear, easily understood manner."

Sentiments I endorse heartily. Sentiments which may be lost on most people because of the way they're phrased. I'd probably word it:

"Whereas, Floridians deserve clear, easily understood communication from their state government, officials and state employees are most effective when they respond to the public's questions and concerns simply and intelligibly."

There: thirty words instead of fifty-four, a 44 percent reduction. All of which rather points out the pervasiveness of the problem. If you can't get an order demanding clear, simple language from government written in a clear, simple way . . . well, I'd say we have a problem.

Or, as politicians like to say, "we have a challenge." Or, as corporate types like to say, "issues have been lately identified."

Clear language is the happy result when people have both the skill to say something and the desire to be understood unambiguously. When the press ridicules people in government for not making sense, we often just assume that government officials want to be understood and fall hilariously short. This is unfair as well as incorrect. In public discourse, blunting meaning is as important as imparting meaning.

The fog does not waft into a conference room because the guy at the microphone lacks verbal skills. Actually, it often is a bravura demonstration of the spokesman's verbal skills. And the reason why he usually earns more than the people hard at work translating his words into normal, understandable language.

These aren't vouchers, they're Opportunity Scholarships. These aren't taxes, they're fees. It's the Anti-Murder Act, not the Prison Building Act. We're not giving up on the rules, we're moving proactively toward the implementation of the new regulatory paradigm, and I'll bop the guy who says otherwise.

Another barrier to clear language in government is the extreme specificity of legal language. Sometimes government is writing for the appellate court, not the public. Add that to the natural desire to seem smart and important, and word inflation can get uproarious.

My favorite example in Florida government was in 2002 when, in writing a ballot summary for a proposed constitutional amendment on the death penalty, the legislature used 579 words to summarize an amendment of 179 words. I used to think summaries were shorter than what they summarize. Live and learn.

So I salute Governor Crist's efforts on behalf of clearer language. It's surely needed. And I salute it all the more heartily, secure in the knowledge that my job translating official pronouncements will not be any less in demand.

January 2007

Event: The Hall of Governors (Living)

At age eighty, Claude Kirk can still be the most quotable guy in the room. Even when the other guys in the room are the Florida governors who came after him. Governors who without exception left the job with far better reviews.

But that's okay. The ol' Claudius Maximus (as they called him back in the '60s) was willing to take credit for their careers, too.

"All these old men were the fruit of my loins," he declared with a sweeping gesture indicating the rest of the stage.

Kirk, who served 1967–1971, was the oldest of the governors present at the Day with the Florida Governors Symposium organized by the Lou

Frey Institute of Politics and Government at the University of Central Florida. Governor Jeb Bush and former Governors Buddy MacKay, Bob Graham, and Reubin Askew were there. Bob Martinez did not attend but sent a video. Wayne Mixson, governor for three days after Bob Graham left for the U.S. Senate, was recovering from an auto accident and was absent.

The effect for any state political wonk was not unlike walking into a live Florida version of Disney's Hall of Presidents.

There was Bush, extolling a goal-directed life and political philosophy while bantering good-naturedly with student protesters who identified themselves as Students for a Democratic Society. ("Is this SDS like the '60s SDS? Wow!")

There was MacKay, governor for three weeks after Lawton Chiles' death, still deep in policy details. He spoke about the need for expanded mediation in juvenile courts (the result of volunteer work), about his change of heart on term limits (he no longer likes them), and mused about the promise of using marginal cost accounting in impact-fee assessment. But he also claimed to have achieved a more laid-back life in Ocala with membership in what he called "the Lake Weir Philosophical Society."

There was Graham, in familiar maroon tie with outlines of the state of Florida, two different color-coded notebooks in his blazer pocket (one yellow, one blue), who talked about the need to "live a balanced life," sang a few bars from the musical "The Fantasticks" (*Plant a radish. Get a radish. Never any doubt!*),and recalled a warm summer day planting a tree with Marjory Stoneman Douglas along a restored section of the Kissimmee River.

There was Askew, who at seventy-seven has the same piercing black eyes that dare anyone not to pay attention to what he's saying, inveighing against the role of big money in government. ("I wasn't given a great chance of winning so was less fettered by special-interest money.")

And last on the program was Kirk, who characteristically took credit for the university where they were standing—"I dug the dirt to start this place!"—and the careers of the others in the room.

"I created turmoil in the Democratic Party and created these governors you see before you . . . these are beautiful children of mine."

Kirk's talk was stand-up comedy for Florida political wonks and history buffs, but here he was probably right. His surprise 1966 victory made him the first Republican governor since Reconstruction. His eventful term and unpredictable behavior in office shook up state government—"I was there ordered by the people to clean up the temple and drive out the moneychangers!—and created rich political opportunities for a rising generation of reform-minded Democrats.

And is this catalytic role in Florida history appreciated? He's glad you asked, because no, it is not. MacKay was governor for less than a month, Kirk complained, "but he has a bigger picture in the hall than I do."

Just another indignity.

March 2006

6 Welcome to the World's Most Famous Beach

"No place whose economy is based on people whooping it up, tipping 20 percent, and floating in seawater is predisposed to be judgmental about people's dress, taste, deportment, or generalized pursuit of happiness."

—*The Darwinian Gardener's Almanac*

CAUTION

• RIP CURRENTS
• SHARKS
• TIME SHARE SALESMEN

Illustration by Bruce Beattie.

A note on "The World's Most Famous Beach"

The alert reader—unaware as always of what a drag he is—may already be wondering about my use of the odd phrase *The World's Most Famous Beach* as a synonym for Daytona Beach. The slogan is a choice bit of 1920s-era advertising zippity-do-dah and has a certain Movietone newsreel sound to it. Until recently, it was on a lot of postcards and city signage. I find it sweetly quaint.

In our more sophisticated modern marketing environment, however, it makes the area's promoters cringe. Which is something else in its favor.

Over the years advertising professionals have come up with many replacements, but they've all sounded blandly generic, like any other place in Florida. *The Fun Coast. Big Beach, Big Fun.* Nothing stuck.

The great thing about the old slogan in its later years is that it has the feel of a local inside joke. When you say it, people from out of town wonder if you're putting them on. And you're not, even though it sounds like a parody of old-time Florida tourism slogans. And it's not like you're bragging or trying to put something over on the listener. For something is not really a lie unless you expect someone to believe it. And we don't. Really.

World's Most Famous Beach car, 1930s. (Photo courtesy of the Halifax Historical Museum, Daytona Beach)

The down side of the slogan is that it can be depressing. Like when they used it on a corroding metal sign arching above a drawbridge. "Gateway to the World's Most Famous Beach," it said. It was a tableau that suggested the entire region's chronic gap between its healthy self-image and what we laughingly call reality.

The slogan has been so long associated with the place that it's hard to pinpoint when it first lodged itself into the local vocabulary. It goes way back. There was a 1919 brochure that carried the slogan, *The World's Famous Ocean Beach*. Pretty close. But it seems to have taken off in the 1920s when the place received worldwide attention for auto speed records set on the beach.

So when you encounter the phrase in these pages, it refers to Daytona Beach, the beaches, and places nearby. It is a slogan, not an actual claim.

And it will be our little joke. Okay?

2007

The dynamic inlet

From a distance the big cranes and orange earth-moving equipment sitting on the beach look like toys left behind in a sandbox by a careless child. They are parked in the sand because work is starting on a project that will reshape the shoreline of Ponce Inlet and try, one more time, to tinker with the natural balance of sand, tide, and sea.

The bulldozers sit next to the vestiges of the red brick foundation of Hotel Inlet Terrace, one of many grand real estate dreams that died with the Florida land boom of the 1920s. Work was hardly under way when the hurricane of 1926 tore it apart. The bricks, newly uncovered by Hurricane Floyd and other recent storms, stretch in a red dotted line into the waves. The hotel was meant to be near the sea, not in the sea.

But figuring out where the sea is supposed to be is no easy calculation. Inlets are not like mountains or lakes. Left to their own devices, they move around. A lot. No two old maps of the inlet show the same soundings. At low tide, when it was silted up, there were periods when people could wade between Ponce Inlet and New Smyrna Beach.

Fixing it is an old idea. "A good channel to the ocean could be made at small expense which could more than repay in five years the entire outlay," pronounced the *Daytona Beach News-Journal*'s venerable ancestor, the *Halifax Journal*, in 1883.

Despite local support for the project, digging an inlet channel would wait until World War II. It looked easy, just an underwater ditch. It didn't work that way. The fact that cranes, Georgia granite, and half-submerged hotel ruins all share the same patch of beach is a pretty good symbol of the vagaries of inlet-shaping.

Jetties were built on both sides of Ponce Inlet in 1972 and shored up in 1998. Still, the shoreline kept changing. In fact, part of the shore inland from the jetty began wearing away at an alarming rate.

"It's a very dynamic inlet," observed Tim Martin, project manager for the Army Corps of Engineers's next plan for fixing the inlet.

Well, that's one way to put it.

He explained that because the inlet's mouth is too wide, the water oscillates between the jetties. The water's movement is eroding the inlet's northwest shoreline.

The new project will extend Ponce Inlet's north jetty westward and build a line of boulders along the shore farther west. The sand near that line of rock eventually will erode, leaving a granite shoreline.

"A hard boundary for the oscillations of the channel," according to Martin.

And what would happen if nature simply took its course?

"It would become an island, sir," Martin said. "The inlet would move north."

Ponce Island. Now, that's one dynamic inlet. So dynamic, it cost $20 million to stabilize between 1972 and 1993. Then another $1 million to dredge in 1994 and more than a million to fix in 1998. The new work is the first $5 million installment of a $10 million project that will include additions to the south jetty in New Smyrna Beach. That's a lot of money to dump into the ocean, but the alternative is Ponce Island.

As dynamic as Ponce Inlet may be, its case is neither unique nor rare.

Of the nineteen inlets on Florida's east coast, seventeen are, as they say in the business, improved. That is, lined with rocks and jetties.

The Army engineers hope this project will do the trick.

"It's been two Band-Aids we've put in place," Martin said. "I do consider this to be the last Band-Aid in the foreseeable future."

"Foreseeable" may be a prudent modifier. The inlet's capriciousness remains the stuff of local legend.

Soon the trucks full of boulders, the cranes, and the bulldozers will start their work, and by this time next year, we'll get to see what the ocean will decide to do next.

October 1999

Postscript: The project is now complete. New Band-Aids are under discussion.

Hard sell on soft sand violates the Beach-Dude Way

The Beach-Dude Way is to hang loose and not hassle anyone. Like all the world's great systems of social philosophy, the Beach-Dude Way has its enemies and detractors. And its newest enemies are giving even its mellowest practitioners pause.

The Beach-Dude Way is a more complex philosophy than apparent on the surface. Take another look at this credo and you will note it has two parts: (1) hang loose; (2) don't hassle anyone. A personal expectation and a related social duty.

There is no sign at the beach entrance instructing people in this. Clearly this is an oversight. As it is, most beach signs violate the spirit of section one of the Way.

The Beach-Dude Way is universal to beaches. It is respected internationally, even in crowded city beaches. You can sit on beaches from Rio to

Miami, shoulder to shoulder in a crowd of sunbathers with skyscrapers behind them and sea before them, and find the folks around you to be determinedly loose, nonaggressive, and nonjudgmental. So powerful is the Beach-Dude Way that it can tame even hard-living urbanites the world over. But it can't deter the march of aggressive free enterprise.

Beachgoers in Florida complain increasingly that they are stalked by enemies of the Beach-Dude Way. They report being hunted by salesmen. And not just any salesmen—timeshare condominium salesmen. Salesmen who are as persistent as panhandlers. As aggressive as telephone swamp-lot peddlers. As impervious to rejection and insult as the most whacked-out cult members.

They disguise themselves as beach-dudes in order to walk among them. Yet they are the very opposite. They are hasslers. Hasslers are what people drive to beaches to escape. The natural enemies of beach dudes.

So as more beach-dozers awake to the smiling faces of pitchmen, new tensions are building on the shore. Tourists are screaming, motel owners are complaining, and chambers of commerce are calling for prudent self-regulation. Beach-dudes, meanwhile, are wading into deeper water and calming themselves down. It is an ugly situation.

The right to privacy, as Louis Brandeis first defined it, is "the right to be left alone." And the beach-dude is as private as a crab. He walks a habitat where the right to be left alone is better respected than in any other public place. Aggressive salespeople are predators in such an environment. Their prey lack the usual natural defenses.

Freely trespassing, the salesmen break the unwritten social compact of the beach. They violate the expectation that beaches exist as hassle-free preserves.

We live in a culture where telephone salespeople call us during dinner, mass mailers fill our mailboxes with sweepstakes entries, and scam artists stuff our e-mail accounts with surefire get-rich-quick schemes. So maybe it's naive to believe we might avoid them simply by walking outdoors.

Perhaps the timeshare hawkers are shoreline trailblazers and we can soon expect magazine-subscription peddlers and insurance sellers to follow their footprints by the surf. Maybe vendors of riptide and shark insurance, too. The door-to-door salesman is being replaced by the outdoor-to-outdoor salesman.

Nature has just become scarier. So this summer I walk the shore with caution. I apply sunscreen and look out for jellyfish, sharks, and time-share salesmen. I block out the drone of low-flying planes trailing advertising banners. I flee the thudding bass of radio boom boxes. I am alerted a mile away to the lawnmower-like aroma of power-skis.

This combination is enough to make me wonder if I should look into the Mountain-Dude Way. I suspect, though, you'd have to wear shoes to live it. That's no good. Besides, I suspect mountain-trail timeshare salesmen are already stuffing flyers and contracts in their backpacks.

Why would someone sell timeshares on a mountaintop? Because it's there.

August 1999

Postscript: Timeshare sales on the beach are now more strictly regulated than when this piece appeared. For that reason, and because I appear a less likely sales prospect now that I'm older, seedier, and my kids won't go to beach with me, I'm seldom approached on the beach.

Good pain at beach run

Maybe it's the time of year. Maybe it's the way people do odd things when they get to a beach. But Daytona Beach's Easter Beach Run always has appealed to people who enter out of sheer impulse.

There are spring breakers who hear about it by accident. Occasional runners who don't race but suddenly decide to give it a go. Former spectators who have encountered the stream of the beach runners in years past and noticed that the vast middle of the field is made up of folks who look like normal people rather than gaunt marathoners or sculpted young athletes. This sight begs the question: why not?

In the great Easter Beach Run tradition, the race Saturday was won by fifteen-year-old Andrew Skidmore, who hadn't heard of the race a week ago, hadn't raced on sand before, and had bought his sneakers a few hours beforehand.

And there was another story of springtime impulse-running in 469th place. That's because, with zero training or warm-up tries, I ran the race for the first time in nearly a decade.

Before the race, the last distance I had run was the length of the newspaper parking lot before a thunderstorm. The last Easter Beach Run that included me was in 1996. People might say I was rusty. I prefer to say I was well-rested.

Running takes more than tolerance to pain and boredom. It takes a connoisseurship of pain and boredom. You tell yourself you know the difference among different kinds of pain and boredom. That you can distinguish "good pain"—the glowing feeling of muscles building and adjusting—from "bad pain"—the feeling that you're about to be updated on your health plan's new restrictions.

Single-parenthood, the time crunch, refusal to follow a schedule, and a general inability to tell good pain from bad pain drove me from the pastime years ago.

Still, there was the beach run. A community-wide event that since 1968 has embraced impulsive runners, invited people who have no business in a race, lured the curious, and tempted private runners out into the open.

While standing at the starting line with the wind blowing rain in my face, this did not seem like one of my better impulsive acts. But that feeling vanished as the group surged forward.

The most exhilarating part of a race is the first hundred yards, when you're effortlessly borne by a wave of people. The worst part is the second hundred yards, when you more accurately assess the situation.

The rain and fog made the halfway turn-around point a surprise that popped out of the mist rather than a landmark to strive for.

Still, my goal of completing the race without medical assistance and arriving there before people started taking down the finish line and going home was accomplished.

As for the people who are actually competent runners, I feel I was doing them a service, too. They need bad runners. People to be ahead of, a crowd to look back at, a field that makes them look good. It sounds far more impressive to win against six hundred bad-to-just-okay people than to win against sixty people in excellent shape.

The trouble with most sports is that sometime during high school, people divide themselves starkly and unalterably into doers and spectators. We are either compulsive, driven competitors or couch potatoes.

There are few events that embrace those who are active-but-marginal while celebrating those who are good-to-amazing. The Easter Beach Run is a rarity in that it does that. You can run it to prove nothing more than that you can still run a few miles without anyone calling an ambulance.

That's good pain.

March 2005

Whose beach? Not easy to answer

Whose beach is it, anyway? And which sands belong to whom? You'd think that since people have been walking this beach for some time, that question would be pretty much worked out by now. Well, it isn't. The good news, though, is that the string of court cases protecting the beach-goers's accustomed rights to walk, fish, and even drive cars on the beach remains unbroken.

The latest was a ruling by Circuit Court Judge J. David Walsh on a particularly aggressive claim of private ownership and control of the beach west of where the sand gets wet. A claim helped along by the Pacific Legal Foundation, a group that sues to promote private property–rights claims.

A group of New Smyrna Beach beachfront landowners filed suit in 2000 asking the court to ban beach driving and force county government to repay them for having allowed cars to drive on their property. Their property being the sand between the mean high waterline and the sand dunes. Or where the sand dunes would be if they were there. The judge turned them down flat.

"The plaintiffs cannot come forth after a century of vehicle access and use and decades after the City of New Smyrna Beach began regulating vehicles on the beach, to complain that their property rights have been abridged," he wrote. In other words, the suit came about a hundred years too late.

Actually, this suit is not just about cars on the beach. For if cars are "trespassing" and "physically invading" the beachfront landowners's sand, then sunbathers, beach walkers, bike riders, and Frisbee throwers are trespassers and invaders, too.

The legal theory is the same. If you're on the beach and your feet are dry, you would likely be trespassing. If you want to go to the beach, buy a condo like everyone else.

The court rejected envelope-pushing property-rights absolutism in favor of the customary uses and the free access to the beach generations of Volusians and visitors have enjoyed. The ability to stroll the beach or throw down a towel somewhere where you won't get wet seems so natural, so right and basic to living in Florida, that it surprises people to discover that there's no constitutional amendment or state statute that unequivocally says "you can't chase people off the dry beach for just hanging out, not even surfers or teenagers." Or words to that effect.

In Florida, being able to stroll on the dry sand has depended on court rulings. Court rulings that talked about fairly abstract legal concepts: "customary uses," "implied dedication," and my personal favorite, "prescriptive easements." Judges know we can be on the beach, but they can differ on just why.

This has made beach-access rulings complex and difficult, with a sometimes breathtaking common-law historical sweep. Definitely not beach reading.

The definitive Florida beach access case remains a 1974 divided Florida Supreme Court ruling (with the appropriately cheesy sounding name *Daytona Beach v. Tona-Rama*), which allowed a sightseeing tower sunk into the beach sand at the base of the Main Street Pier in Daytona Beach to stay put. Even though a divided court also found it shouldn't have been built there in the first place.

As a dry-sand beach walker, I hope this legal tradition continues. But that's a lot to ask for. We are living in a time when increasingly conservative appellate courts are very receptive to more absolute claims based on the sanctity of property rights.

It would not take but a few rulings by more activist conservative appellate courts to create long stretches of private beaches on sand that used to be everybody's. What courts grant, courts can take away.

For now at least, that tide has been rolled back and these footprints on dry sand are perfectly legal, not to mention customary.

October 2005

Floridans, Volusians, Ormandetti

If you have the misfortune to live in Afghanistan, you are an Afghan, not an Afghani. Afghani is what they call the paper that you'd want to convert to real money once you slip across the border into Pakistan. Yet the people who live there are Pakistanis, not Pakistans.

Why don't place/people names make sense? I am a Floridian. Not a Floridanian. So why aren't people from Jordan calling themselves Jordians instead of Jordanians?

The estimable late editor of the *Daytona Beach News-Journal*, Herbert M. Davidson, was offended by the mellifluous illogic of the word *Floridian*.

"We are not from Floridia," he declared and insisted that his paper run *Floridan* as the state personal noun. A word that has the additional advantage of being a letter shorter and thus saving space in news stories and headlines.

Like so many other progressive ideas, this efficient and pleasant adjective was opposed by the Florida legislature. The Florida House of Representatives in 1925 declared by resolution that "the word *Floridian* is musical, poetical, euphonious, and easily roll[s] off the tongue." And who should know more about music and poetry than the Florida House?

Contrariwise, it found *Floridan* to be "harsh, unmusical, and unjustified by precedent." Take that. The Senate, rising to its role as the more deliberative body, refused to take up the matter.

But by the time the House had spoken, *Floridian* had already won the usage wars. That still left a lot of similar problems on the local level.

I tell people I'm a Daytonan. This is easy to say and true mostly. More than fifty Florida towns and cities end in *Beach*, and like everyone else who lives near a beach, Daytonans (not Daytonians) drop the word. Just as New Smyrnans and Ormandites do.

Actually I live in Ormond Beach, but we are Ormandites there even though it sounds like a mineral deposit and can confuse the listener. I don't know why my town went that route except to avoid being Ormanders or Ormondidians. Personally I think we should have been the Ormandetti. We would have been fearsome.

DeLandites made the same mistake as the Ormandites. Delandacians would roll off the tongue but would be murder on headline writers.

Before I was an Ormonder, I was a Holly Hillian. I didn't like that name, either. "I am of the Hill People," I would say if asked.

Like the Hill People, the Inlet People keep both words in their town name. Instead of calling themselves Ponceros, Poncepolitans, or something cool, people from Ponce Inlets are generally Ponce Inleters.

Worse is the plight of people in of Daytona Beach Shores. They can't drop anything or they'd be Daytonans. They are the Shore Dwellers, without a name of their own.

But we are all Volusians, and that positively rolls off the tongue. Except that it makes you sound a little like a citizen of the Federation of Planets. (A Federali? Federalist?)

"Volusian, not Venusian," I explain when people react oddly.

The people with the best group names are the ones who unmoor themselves entirely from their place names. The Hoosiers. The Tar Heels. The Cariocas who know better than to construct anything from a city name that takes up three words.

These are rich designations with mysterious origins deep in history. Maybe the lack of good names is just one of the drawbacks of living in a place where people have not had generations to ponder such matters.

November 2001

Beach signs mark runners' painful paths

There is one mile of firm and even beach between the spot where the "Welcome to Ormond Beach" sign used to be and the flagpole behind the green house that always flies the flag.

The next mile is trickier. It ends where the motel telephone booth used to be. Roughly ten feet south of a brick barbecue grill.

If you are ambitious and plan an eight-mile round trip, you look next for the spot where the tables begin, just south of the coquina clock next to the Adam's Mark Hotel. But at that distance, it shouldn't matter if you spot yourself a few feet.

Thankfully the days of such raw estimates are ending. Volusia County is erecting mile markers.

Each has a cheerful orange sun with a mile number at its center. Mile 1 North is near the Flagler border. Mile 26 North is at Ponce Inlet jetty. The numbers start anew on the south side of the inlet and end at Mile 10 South, near the Canaveral National Seashore.

My usual course is centered near Mile 10 North and Mile 11 North. I've long ago given up on running. Around the time my kids became teenagers, I mysteriously found I no longer had the energy or time. Besides, when I began believing it was vital to know the exact point where a motel phone booth used to be set in concrete, it was easy to suspect this endeavor was getting too compulsive.

Perhaps with mile markers, I might have lasted longer. My legs cramp up at the thought. Now I merely walk. I keep my pace brisk enough to enjoy cardiovascular benefits and slow enough to carry a drink without the toy umbrella falling out.

Mile 10 is a good starting point. Not too different from one of my old running courses. A course that finished its first quarter near the warning sign about the shipwreck of the Nathan B. Cobb. Usually at that point in a run, I would take any mention of wrecks entirely too personally. I discontinued that particular route.

Mile 11 North is near the lifeguard station. Which is most convenient should one lapse into unconsciousness near a run's midpoint.

But now, as a mellow beach walker instead of a driven runner, I take Mile 11 North in stride.

The mile posts are certain to be a hit. People always want to know precisely where they are and how far it would be if they would just turn around and go back.

This is not an unmixed blessing. Is a beach really a place that cries out for linear measurement? Are we so goal-driven that we need an exact spot to turn and hit the lap buttons on our digital watches? Will people still cheat on distances without the excuse of underestimating where the missing city-limits or telephone booth sign used to be? The answers to those questions are "yeah, well, probably" and "why even ask?"

I looked at the footprints near Mile 10 North and saw the firm, regular, rippled tread of a determined runner. The prints came seven feet short of the mile marker, then turned on a dime and headed back north.

Someone's cutting corners here. You're supposed to touch the mile markers now that we have them or you are only cheating yourself.

That's what all the running books say. Running books are written to encourage people's deepest compulsive tendencies. As a reformed runner, bent on tormenting thin people, I would have shouted something along those lines to the owner of those footprints.

As the kind of person who feels reassured every time I see the phrase *you are here* on a map, I know I will love these signs. On the other hand, the beach is a wonderful place not to know exactly where you are for a while.

April 2000

Downshifting to one speed

Let's start with definitions. A beach cruiser has fat tires. A beach cruiser has one speed. And although all beach cruisers have fat tires and one choice of gear, all bicycles with fat tires and one choice of gear are not beach cruisers.

These two things are merely the core of the definition. The rest is aesthetics and philosophy and open to debate. Fat tires. One speed. Headed toward the beach.

There are those who will attempt to pass off any heavy-framed bicycle as a beach cruiser. Laughable, dude. Do not try to call some old mountain bike a beach cruiser because it has fat tires and is rusty. You ever see a derailleur coated in coquina sand? It is not pretty. In action it sounds like somebody working on a bag of corn chips.

Same goes for hand brakes. They will rust inside of two summers. (The age of beach cruisers is determined summer to summer. I thought everybody knew this.) The rusty metal will come unwound, stab you in the leg, and you'll die of tetanus. Yes, you could. A beach cruiser is meant to be in the elements. A beach cruiser has coaster brakes.

I now own something close to the Platonic ideal of a beach cruiser. It cost $35, but it was worth it.

It has enough rust to possess character, but not enough to threaten its being or mine. And it has a wide old seat with big springs like a mattress. Not one of those racing-bike seats that looks like a garden spade.

The bike makes cranky noises going uphill and has oversized handlebars. But most of all, it actually sees the beach.

Many so-called beach cruisers are sold nowhere near water. This is mere marketing. A renaming of a newsboy-style bike to make it palatable to adults. An attempt to cash in on inland people's beach fantasies. Nice try. It is an homage to the concept but should not be mistaken for the real thing.

In most places a beach cruiser is transportation to and from the beach. Around the beach. To the edge of the beach. Volusia County's beach is a rarity in that it has been a hard-sand bike path for more than century. There are few places on the planet where a beach cruiser may better fulfill its potential than right here.

People think of a beach cruiser as summer transport, which it is. Particularly those models with surfboard carriers. The kind that look like small sailboats when pedaled to the waves. But for me, early autumn beach riding is best. The beach hasn't yet narrowed for winter. Fewer people. Less car-dodging.

Some people might add fewer witnesses. Because nobody looks graceful on a beach cruiser. Particularly in a society so narrow-minded as to consider one-speed bikes strictly for those under twelve.

This does not concern me. It is a rule of the beach that all accessories used or worn in sight of water are pretty much okay. Among goofy hats, nakedness, weird sunglasses, and nose coverings, the addition of a one-speed bike cannot have a discernable effect on personal dignity. Comparatively speaking.

I described my new find to an old friend and got back an e-mail asking if I was going to buy a bell, baskets, and handlebar streamers, too. This was not a helpful suggestion, but contained, on closer reading, elements of sarcasm.

Not everyone is ready for the beach-cruiser concept and a return to no-frills, rusty-frame biking. We are too easily impressed with superbikes with aircraft-metal frames. We have forgotten the simple pleasures of bike riding in our awe of sports engineering.

I did not rise to these jibes. The beach cruiser is antifashion-by-the-sea and dares to be unapologetically geeky. And a basket? Not a bad idea, but really, isn't that what milk crates are for?

September 2003

Stripes by the posthurricane beach

If you walk along the beach here this week you'll notice three wavy lines on most sea walls. The bottom line is where sand dunes used to be before the hurricanes took them away. The next line is where the surf took off the paint like a sandblaster and exposed past paint coats or bare concrete. The last line is where the highest tides rubbed, sanded, and scraped, discoloring the walls but leaving the paint.

The bottom stripe is alarming and wide. Even though you are walking along a noticeably skinnier beach, this is the line that says, "Right here. This is the spot where the sand came up just five weeks ago."

It's near this layer that you'll sometimes see old sets of concrete beach steps, long disused, that have been uncovered by the storms. Weathered and jutting from the sand, they look like something unearthed by archaeologists, an entrance to a forgotten temple. Sea oats were growing above them at the start of summer.

And they remind you that, however rough the beach looks now, there have been other times when the dunes retreated like this. Those concrete stairs were poured there because somebody thought that was where the sand should be. But sand, as we know, is indifferent to such plans.

The first line is about nature. The second line is about people. The second line exposes old paint colors. It shows how tastes and sign ordinances have changed. This line exposes phone numbers and hand-painted hotel logos—speeding cars, birds, smiling suns, and red italic letters giving the names of motels as they were three or four owners ago. The colors are often more garish. Graffiti of a decade ago has magically reappeared.

Sometimes you come across an uncovered hotel name within a foot or so of where the dune used to be. People don't paint signs at ankle level. Somebody painted that because they thought the sand would stay four feet under the letters. But sand, as we know, is indifferent to sign painters.

The third line gives you a small idea of the high-water mark of the storm. Remember that for later.

Walking the beach last weekend was a bittersweet experience. It was the first normal beach weekend in more than a month, and people were out in numbers to enjoy it.

It felt good even though the sand was redder and darker and softer than the usual silver, hard-packed promenade. Even though the beach was too narrow for traffic. Even though the surf was still rough enough to be more attractive to surfers than swimmers. Even though the familiar sounds of kids and waves and shore birds were punctuated with squeal of power saws and the thunk of roofers's nail guns firing nearby.

Beachcombers found yard plants and parts of houses and decking among the usual seaweed and wash-up at the high-tide line. The buried asphalt foundations of the beach's car ramps are dug up and exposed and look from a distance like wet beached whales.

But most dramatic were the missing dunes at the three-striped sea walls and the accompanying dune walkovers with stairs that end in mid-air. Sand, as we know, is indifferent to wooden stairs. We like to think we can dump a pile of sand next to a hotel's sea wall and it will stick around. But the stripes and the walkovers in the air and excavated stairways suggest anything done here is done strictly for the short term.

Sand and wind and waves decide the long term. The long term is a cycle of building up and washing away. Sand banked in dunes and spent in storms.

The long-term cycle is we know this and then forget it. That we're impressed with the lines, paint over the lines, and forget the lines. Then we decide sand will stay put, and the cycle begins again.

October 2004

Sea-beaners prize the pods others pass by

This is one of those two-kinds-of-people things. Most people walk along a beach and never notice those pebble-looking things in the sand. A few people do, though. They pick them up and put them in their pockets. They polish them, put the cool ones on shelves, look them up in out-of-print books, and somehow connect them to the barely understood workings of ocean dynamics, nature, life, and the universal order.

These are the people who know better than to dismiss them as spots of beach tar, sea trash, or shell pieces. These are sea-beans. Floating seeds from coastal plants that wash up from distant coasts.

I was among the sea-beaners last week. The beaners had gathered at Melbourne Beach for the Second Annual Sea-Bean Symposium.

When I got there, close to twenty people were milling around a large table at the Melbourne Beach community center. This was the finish line of the bean-a-thon competition, and they were dumping bags of beans on the table while experts sorted through them. At the height of the count, the table held the proverbial hill of beans. Along with an elaborate floating flare and a toilet seat that, from the barnacles attached, appeared to have spent some time at sea.

"Mostly mangrove seeds," Cathie Katz said. Then, lowering her voice to me conspiratorially, added, "I don't consider them real sea-beans."

A lot of golf ball beans and blister pods, too. The winner of this year's bean-a-thon collected 3,394 beans in only a few hours.

Katz is the editor of a newsletter devoted to the dissemination of sea-bean lore, *The Drifting Seed*. About four hundred people subscribe worldwide.

When she talks, her eyes, framed by shaggy blonde bangs, often crinkle in barely suppressed laughter. She sometimes bounces on the balls of her feet when she's standing in one place, which is seldom.

Katz exudes energy when she speaks about her projects, writing, and life concerns: whether it's her favorite writers (Diane Ackerman, Jack Rudloe), her dyslexia, all-weather beach walking, the art of knowing when a hurricane will be serious, or the mechanics of polishing sea-beans for jewelry. You must pick up your pace if you want to walk with her. She says she doesn't really remember when her interest—others might say obsession—with sea-beans began.

"It must be genetic," she says. "There's just something different about us." A two-kinds-of-people thing. The beans are either something you step on or something that can halt your walk every few yards to check out a new find.

In her workaday, away-from-the-beach, non-bean life, she is a technical writer for Johns Hopkins University. The university is closing its Florida office, a move that soon will leave her out of a job. She sees this, however, as a push to move on to better things.

"It's like Joseph Campbell says, 'follow your bliss.' I'm just following my bliss, which is not working with missiles right now."

Her bliss right now is centered on beans and beaches. It's led her to write and illustrate a series of books on natural Florida. *The Nature of Florida's Waterways* and *The Nature of Florida's Beaches* came first. Packed with hundreds of small, black-and-white illustrations, the books are busy, fact-filled, silly, and profound.

Following her bliss from sea-beans to the source of the definitive sea-bean guide led her to Charles R. Gunn, a North Carolina botanist, sea-bean guru, and coauthor of *World Guide to Tropical Drift Seeds and Fruits*. Their meeting led to the newsletter and the sea-bean symposiums.

"I looked in his office and saw just hundreds of letters from people all over the world. They all said, 'I found this bean on the beach, it looks like this. Can you tell me what it is?' I knew then I wasn't alone."

And she's not.

Shore gatherers are the most observant of beachgoers. Shell finders always seem to be more romanticized. But anyone who can pick up a hamburger bean and understand something of the Gulf Stream, Brazilian shoreline ecology, nature, and the universe has enjoyed a profitable day on the beach.

Myself, I don't know beans. On my walks I tend to watch the shore walkers as much as the shore. Now I suspect I should pay more attention to the sand beneath my feet.

"There is something magical about these beans," Katz told me. And I'm inclined to believe her.

October 1997

Postscript: The Sea-Bean Symposium is still an annual event. Cathie Katz died of cancer in 2001. She wrote the drafts of her books on index cards. This was what she wrote on one of the cards that year: "I loved the urgency. I loved the compelling nature of the days. I was luckier than anyone deserved—to have this joy of living fully for the first time, day after day without knowing how many days were left. It made each one the biggest, best, and brightest I'd ever experienced." She was fifty-two.

At beach equinox, all balances

The autumn equinox is the beach equinox, too. A time of perfect balance.

Autumn—at least the generic autumn you see on calendars with those weird, exotic pages of red barns and impossible trees with burgundy and gold leaves—officially begins on one of two days of the year when light and darkness claim perfect halves of the day. The rest of the year, for consumers of daylight, is downhill from then.

The autumn equinox is a bigger deal the farther north you go. In places where days get short enough to leave you feeling like you live in a mine around February, it's a real wake-up call. Here, who notices?

Well, I do. At least as it relates to the beach. The fall equinox is when all the forces affecting the beach—tide, temperature, traffic, and tourist season—are in the right equilibrium. At least if you don't own a motel or sell T-shirts.

It's a time when the tourist season is at low ebb, yet the water is still warm. It's a time when you can walk the beach in the afternoon and seldom step aside for an oncoming car, yet when the shore is still populated enough for a reasonable amount of people-watching.

When it's still placid enough for beach clothes. Yet with enough incipient fall storminess for the kind of waves that beckon surf dudes to skip school. And well before the time when the waves grow so rambunctious that they slam against sea walls and leave room for only the most determined walkers.

These are days when an afternoon walker will find himself putting his sunglasses away halfway through a walk. But he won't yet need his headlights for the drive home.

It's when interesting things—surf-polished fish bones, Brazilian tropical seeds, weird fish lures, and pieces of boats—begin washing up on shore. But well before the season of having to climb over mounds of seaweed in soft sand.

When evening winds blow cool and northerly, chasing away summer's fog of dead humidity that can steam your glasses before you make it all the way out of the car. But it's not yet the season for north winds that make you lean forward for half of your walk. When there's wind enough for kites, but not enough to feel sand in your teeth after talking to somebody.

And a time well away from tourist events. In the lull between the departure of summer visitors and the arrival of the snowbirds.

And since we're conditioned to think of beach walks as one more thing gone with school's premature start in August or at least with the post-Labor Day quickening pace of living, September beach time has the tang of a guilty pleasure. You aren't supposed to be here. This is autumn. We are supposed to be back to work this time of year. Anyone on the beach on equinox week has to suspect they are getting away with something. And we are.

Okay, I hear the objections murmured in the back of the room. So if this is really such a perfect time for beach folks, why is the beachside emptying out, Mr. Beach Expert?

There is no answer. Somehow people have convinced themselves that summer is over. I do not know why.

I'm surprised people don't make a point of going to beaches at exactly this time of year. I would if I had to live somewhere inland and away. Still, if they did, then this wouldn't be such a perfect season, would it? The balance of sparse, but not deserted, beach would be destroyed.

For that reason, this is something September beach walkers should just keep to themselves. Just forget I said any of this.

September 2002

January beach census

A January like this is a test for the year-round beach walker. A trial that culls the fair-weather beachgoer. That eliminates sunny-day naturalists. That exposes the surf-shop surf dude.

I salute you, wind-chill beachcombers! But without taking my hands out of my jacket pockets.

This week, when low temperatures have been moving without pause from the weather page to the record book, and the wind violates the posted 15-mph beach speed limit, the shore is pretty empty.

But not deserted. No, you can still find the real shore dwellers, the people who will not be chased inside. They are the bold, the driven, the climatically clueless, and a few Canadians.

Most Floridians have forgotten or never learned the basics of dressing themselves in this temperature range. The results tend toward extremes. Some overreact with exotic frostwear sprung from deep storage. Others indulge in denial, declaring that because this is Florida, a sweatshirt must, by definition, handle any climatic exigency.

Myself, I suggest your basic Bike Week leather jacket. My children ridicule this as an affectation reeking of midlife crisis. I don't care. It's warm and much cheaper than a red convertible.

Warm even at this time. When the wind whips up at dusk and the fishing boats come in close to shore and turn on their lights. And despite wind and cold that make my eyes tear up, I'm not alone.

There are people on this beach undeterred by weather maps that color the state blue. Their instinct to walk seaward is unquestioned even when the sky has a look that in other latitudes would send people digging through garages for snow shovels.

I find within a single mile:

1. A kite flyer who won't chase his craft no matter how treacherous the wind, no matter how threateningly the kite dips. This is an aficionado who keeps it all in the wrists and arms, otherwise motionless except to retrieve it each time it nosedives.

2. A teenager, sockless in sneakers and wearing baggy shorts that just cover his knees. He's not going to pay any more attention to the seasons than to the parent who told him to wear a jacket.

3. A determined older jogger who looks like one of those children's puzzles in which you have to match the top and the bottom of all the figures, but which always ends up with one scrambled, the monkey's legs showing beneath the ballerina's torso. Above, he wears a thick sweat-shirt and high-tech-fiber jacket zipped to his throat, the picture of cold-weather athleticism. Below the waist, it's the same shorts he would run in on any sunny Florida day.

4. A woman wearing a coat with a hood. And under the coat with a hood is a sweatshirt with a hood pulled up under the coat's hood. And a cap under the hood which is pulled up under the coat's hood. She is as round as a spaceman with layers of clothing and walks at an angle as though moving uphill. But she will complete a walk on the surf's edge.

5. A young athlete running at a zigzag rather than working entirely against the wind. T-shirted, he concedes only long pants to the weather. Onlookers gasp.

6. And me.

That's the census. A half-dozen people, but it proves my point. An ur-ban beach will remain alive and populated under all conditions.

I have walked this stretch of sand at the edge of a hurricane and have still seen other people. It has been a kind of hot that fries you in your sun-screen but all the more crowded for it. During thunderstorms lifeguards must chase people away and make them to go home.

But lifeguards or rain or wind will not make them stay home. This is the beach hard core who won't give up their shoreline movements. If I weren't doing it myself, I might think it was dumb. Instead I just declare us the true beach people and break into a run to get back in the car.

January 2001

The blank monument by the sea

For most of Volusia County's cities, January is when power changes hands. Plaques are presented, thank-you speeches are made, often sincerely, and new nameplates are installed. Sometimes the National Guard is called, but only once to my knowledge. Still, the fact that it happened at all should remind us not to take boring local politics for granted.

It happened in 1937, a time when news stories identified local politicians, with no other elaboration, as "Ring" or "Anti-Ring," as though these were political parties. The Ring was one of those interlocking political alliances that might be found in any rural Southern county. But in Volusia County, its opposition was more persistent and its reaction more extreme than elsewhere.

The Ring sometimes was more formally called the "Courthouse Ring." Sometimes the "Whitehair Ring" for Francis Whitehair, the Ring's central figure. Sometimes the "Whitehair-Fish Ring" adding Bert Fish. And occasionally the "Fish-Whitehair-Armstrong Ring" which added to the constellation longtime Daytona Beach mayor, Ernest Armstrong.

And it was under Armstrong that things got most out of hand. It happened in the last weeks of David Sholtz's term as governor. A New Dealer and local reformer, Sholtz was the only Florida governor from Volusia County.

The mayor suspected Sholtz, a Ring foe, would remove him from office. To thwart him, Armstrong resigned and turned the office over to his wife, Irene.

A neat trick, but it only delayed Sholtz, who on January 1, 1937, removed Mrs. Armstrong from office along with the rest of the City Commission, and appointed a whole new city government. The governor charged the commissioners with malfeasance, misfeasance, neglect of duty, and incompetence. The city, he said, had illegally spent $200,000 more than its budget. About $2.2 million in today's dollars. A breathtaking sum in the depths of the Great Depression.

Mrs. Armstrong, however, was not one to go quietly. She barricaded herself in City Hall with policemen and deputized garbage collectors armed with riot guns and pistols. City records were carted off to waiting garbage trucks and just disappeared.

It was like a bad movie. Here are the headlines in the *Daytona Beach Evening News*:

CITY HALL AN ARMED FORTRESS . . .

COPPERS HOLD RIOT GUNS AT WINDOWS

'Mayor Irene' Commands Police to Occupy City Hall, Resists Expulsion Edict Charging Incompetency.

Sholtz responded by mobilizing the National Guard. The standoff lasted five days. In the national news coverage that ensued, Daytona Beach became a national symbol of small-town corruption and politics out of control. You can't buy publicity like that.

"It will soon blow over," was the headline in an *Evening News* editorial late in the crisis. And strangely, it did.

The next governor refused to reinstate the removals, and the courts held for the Armstrongs. Mrs. Armstrong gave the job back to her husband that March, and he died the next year. Armstrong's allies and the vestiges of the Ring drifted in and out of power for another two decades.

There is, near the Bandshell, a fitting nonmonument to the whole sorry affair. An amoebalike coquina rock on top of a coquina pedestal with an empty spot where a plaque should be. It was planned as a memorial to Armstrong, but the motion to put up a plaque and name the Bandshell after him in 1938 died in a 3–2 vote.

Politics today are squeaky clean compared with the Ring's time. And maybe that's what the stone should memorialize: the day the city's politics degenerated to the point of drawn guns. One plaque could show garbage trucks hauling off public records. Another might show riot guns pointing from the windows of old City Hall.

It would be a useful monument because we take for granted smooth transfers of power, open government records, and decisions made in the sunshine. It just wasn't always so.

Plus, the monument without a plaque confuses the tourists and looks a little weird.

January 2000

Last call at the bumper cars

The line for the bumper cars was seventeen people deep. Kids and parents were even queuing up for the Himalaya. That's right, the Himalaya, a mini-ride usually disdained by kids over ten. The littlest kids were appearing fast enough to keep the merry-go-round, way in back, spinning.

And the video games? Mostly dark and unplugged. Even the operational ones were largely ignored. Rides were what people came for, and tonight the rides were free. Even the $3.50 bumper cars. Because Midway Fun Center was closing after a half century.

Midway, along with other businesses on the block, will make way for a multimillion-dollar, beachside-redevelopment project that promises beachside condos and timeshares. Restaurants, too, and not the kind where a guy wearing a stained apron and tattoos above his knuckles throws down pizza on a limp paper plate. And shops that might sell something other than T-shirts. Construction will start as soon as next summer.

But this night was not about the future. The future is vague and uncertain in its details. Not everyone's entirely sure they'll be welcomed in it. This night was about the past.

People who hadn't gone to The Boardwalk in ages, people who may have never taken their kids there (too seedy, so dirty, and those awful panhandlers!) turned up. With kids. With cameras. Amazed the bumper cars were still there. Looking around and pointing at the weathered signs of businesses and rides long gone. Calculating where the old rides stood.

The Boardwalk has been on a slide since, oh, name your date: the 1960s? the '70s? Since the Ferris wheel was taken down? Since the Bullet stopped spinning and the miniature golf course on the roof closed and the little wooden windmill blew off in a thunderstorm?

But on this last night, with people milling around and kids screaming and laughing, and even the panhandlers seeming cleaned up and less insistent . . . it felt dreamlike. Like stepping back many summers ago.

A summer night when the Tilt-a-Whirl and Ferris wheel might complete the evening. (But not the Bullet. I will not go on the Bullet. Even on a dare.) And the tickets would be bought only after rounds of Skee-Ball with wooden balls that had a satisfying heft and rolled into play with a fine, hard rumble.

The tourist-town seediness of The Boardwalk was always part of its attraction. Amusement park seediness helps impart the feeling that you're someplace you're not supposed to be. Which can give it the sheen of a forbidden pleasure.

The purpose of a carnival ride is to give the illusion of danger, even while assuring people they're safe when the bar clanks down in front of their seats. The seediness nearby works like that, too. Providing the illusion of a place more dangerous and colorful than it is. A pleasurable sensation if you're fourteen or so.

Eventually, though, The Boardwalk started looking bad even by arcade and amusement-park standards. The weathered-face panhandlers, bearded and tattooed like pirates, blended with the general ambience a little too well.

When police stepped up patrols it had the odd effect of being less, rather than more, reassuring. They were like seeing an ambulance parked by the Bullet. It suggested things were more serious than they should be.

But this night you could forget all that. Forget why the city is set on seeing the place made over. Forget a future without bumper cars.

It was a warm night filled with the sounds of metal wheels on metal tracks, songs competing through loud speakers, and kids getting completely out of hand. Until 9:00 p.m. when the Midway's lights went out and the doors rolled shut.

August 2006

 7 The great Florida myth

"Places that already know what they are
creep me out."

—*The Darwinian Gardener's Almanac*

Concrete Alligator, DeBary. (Photo by Mark Lane.)

Plea to visitors: Please don't borrow
our carnivorous reptiles

Despite the smiling face at the front desk and the pronouncements of the nearest chamber of commerce, any tourist town is at heart ambivalent about its guests. They drive around lost. They make fun of the way we talk. And when they eat out they take all the pink packets of sweetener from the table.

And they keep trying to steal our carnivorous reptiles. Just last week police charged a North Carolina man with making off with an alligator that had been minding its own business in a lagoon at Congo River Miniature Golf.

Daytona Beach Shores officers said they apprehended the man in the parking lot of his hotel Monday. According to the police report, he was found in the singularly incriminating—not to mention awkward—act of holding the gator's mouth closed. Something that whether legally or illegally done falls unambiguously under the heading "don't try this at home." He was charged with alligator poaching and petty theft.

Why does this sort of thing appear in a newspaper? Alligator grabs tourist isn't news. Tourist grabs alligator—that's news.

Congo River is an African-themed miniature golf course in Daytona Beach Shores. It has lots of utility poles lashed together with ropes, paintings of shields and spears, and a zebra-striped plane fuselage sitting out back. Very colorful.

Its sign out front says it all:

BEST MINI GOLF
IN DAYTONA
LIVE GATOR

This is the second time the sign's closing line attracted the wrong element. Only last year two tourists were arrested after alligator-napping one of the resident reptiles and letting it loose in a motel pool.

Folks, this is a bad idea. Bad for the alligator. Bad for the people involved in the transportation. Bad for the pool boy. Next time someone says to you, "Hey, let's go get a gator and set it loose in the pool!" just say no.

Friends don't let friends bring alligators back to the motel. Consider this a public service announcement.

The persistence of senseless alligator-related tourist crime illustrates something most observers have long suspected about Florida tourism. People don't come here despite the stories they've heard about dangerous wildlife and Nature Run Amok. People come here *because* of the weird stories they've heard about dangerous wildlife and Nature Run Amok.

And if the intrepid traveler does not encounter sharks, poisonous snakes, bears, or alligators? Well, he'll just go out and snatch one himself. Heck, you think we went all this way just to get stinkin' T-shirts?

So remember this the next time you worry that our tourism economy might suffer because of press accounts of shark attacks, killer bees, lightning strikes, alligator attacks, swamp beast sightings, hurricanes, or giant sinkholes eating the interstate. You can't buy publicity like this. It encourages extreme tourism.

The thing that really threatens to kill tourism is that we're threatening to become too much like everywhere else. That's what I lie awake worrying about at night. At least when I'm not hearing odd, thrashing sounds in the bushes out back.

October 2002

Giant monster spider welcome at the front door

The golden orb weaver spider that lived next to the front door of my house died sometime during the Fourth of July thunderstorm. It lived a good life.

It lived a long life by spider standards: about a month's worth of summer days. It always had lots of stuff in its web. It perished operatically during a dramatic thunderstorm complete with nearby lightning strikes and branches falling from trees.

The spider leaves behind an imposing web about as big as I am. It looks as if it could catch birds, squirrels, and smaller children.

Yeah, yeah, if I paid more attention to the house, the web would never have grown this imposing. But by the time I got around to noticing the monster web a few weeks ago, it had grown too large, too amazing to consider destroying. Besides, I wasn't entirely sure a broom would be adequate for the job.

I wondered if it might get even bigger if I held off. So I held off. A simple-minded awe of nature and high-minded spirit of scientific inquiry combined to make web removal seem wrong on a lot of levels.

Besides, the whole display had a certain utility. It kept salesmen and religious proselytizers from the door. There's something about a web the size of a person that gives a house a forbidding, haunted quality. You think twice before knocking on a strange door when there's a spider the size of a squirrel looking over your shoulder.

And I like to believe it gave the home a certain connection with the Great Florida Myth. Part of the Great Florida Myth is that backyard nature here grows luxuriant, out-of-control, and is often dangerous. Not like normal places.

The state myth reminds you that this is a place where the earth beneath your feet might collapse into deep sinkholes that grow like living things. That this is the lightning-strike and shark-bite center of the nation. That we are a place of poodle-eating reptiles and snakes that pop out of nowhere. Naturally such a land has spiders the size of squirrels.

The golden orb weaver, or banana spider, (*Nephila clavipes*) fits into the state story very nicely. At least the females, which are huge and yellow and striped and spotted. The males are smaller and look like regular old garden spiders. The females usually eat them after mating.

There's something about discovering a five-inch spider hovering at face level that brings out the primal in a person. More than one visitor by the front door has let out an involuntary gasp or just the start of a scream.

The frightening of young people and guests did not prompt me to go at the web with an ax and propane torch. On the contrary, it encouraged me to keep it around. Here was something that added an undeniable element of drama to the front entrance to my home—the part of the house where, all the home magazines and real estate agents tell me, the strongest first impressions are manufactured.

But now the spider's gone, and it's just a matter of time before the web gets unacceptably raggedy. And instead of threatening us with thoughts of nature out of control, the empty web threatens us with the thought that spiders and their summers do not last long. Even for the biggest and scariest creatures in the yard that dine on their boyfriends.

And I'd rather take on the dismantling of a giant, squirrel-catching spider web than meditate on that seasonal truth.

July 2004

Palmetto bugs at first sight

"It was as big as my hand and just looked at me like, 'What do you think you're doing here at this hour?!'"

As I listened to this story, I realized I had heard it before. The story is New Resident Discovers Florida's Amazing Indoor Insect Life. The tale has a myriad of domestic settings, sketched according to the teller's particular dramatic techniques. The principal character always appears suddenly but in a wonderful variety of situations. I never tire of hearing it.

The synopsis of this version went like this: a man, unable to sleep, visits his impeccably clean kitchen in the early hours of the morning and finds *he is not alone.* He is confronted by a giant, winged cockroach that appears exasperatingly unalarmed at his presence. Scurrying is beneath it.

"Well, how big was it?" I asked in the nonchalant tone of scientific inquiry.

"Seriously, this big," asserted the narrator, stretching his thumb and index finger as far apart as they could bend.

"That's a palmetto bug," I told him. "A small one but maybe it will grow."

"Not this one, I assure you."

First contact with a palmetto bug is a defining event in an immigrant's slow transformation into a Floridian. To urban types, used to little German cockroaches that scurry at the faint sound of approaching feet, the first appearance of a brown bug the size of a hubcap is like living a scene from the movie *Alien*. Most remember their first sighting years afterward.

The palmetto bug's size, arrogant demeanor, and resistance to countermeasures have taken on mythic proportions in the Sunshine State and are matters of perverse state pride. The jokes are many and tiresome. You could put a saddle on one. The ones in Miami carry guns. They check out of Roach Motels leaving ugly notes about the service. They kill armadillos and drag them to the side of the road so people will think cars hit them.

How big do they get? Glad you asked. Bigger than a breadbox. Bigger than a salami. The size of small cats. Scientists were sent to measure the biggest ones ever spotted but were never head from again. We don't know how big they get because the government won't tell us about the ones found near Crystal River Nuclear Plant.

"I guess I'll have to spray," my friend said.

Spray. Always the first response. Denial: I won't see one like that again. Then it's guilt: if I only kept the kitchen cleaner. Then it's attack: spray, poison, bomb, kill.

Doesn't work. It barely keeps them at bay. It only makes them angry.

Then there's the last stage: acceptance. Acceptance comes slowly. Roach-loathing is something deep and primal. It comes from prehistoric times when terrier-sized palmetto bugs roamed the jungles in search of primeval leftovers.

Many people never overcome it. But for some lucky people there comes a day when they flip on a bathroom light, spot a palmetto bug the size of a shoe, and see, if not a wonder of evolution, at least nature only accidentally intruding, and anyway they're too tired or hungover or weary of seeing the things to fight them for dominance.

One day your heart won't pound anymore. You'll find yourself saying to the bug, "If you'll please make a small effort to move somewhere I can't see you, I'll promise not to chase you and make noises." That's the day you've finally acclimated yourself to Florida.

After all, this climate is made for them, not us. We're the ones who need air conditioners, sunscreen, and bottled water. Everything's already fine with the palmetto bugs, just the way they are.

After you're okay with this, you've earned the right to be amused at other people's tales of insect terror and to scare the tourists with stories you thought up. You're home now.

October 1990

Lightning hits home

Lightning in cartoons and children's drawings always looks like a jagged dagger, issuing in a single point from a burnt-marshmallow cloud. This is the way I imagined it when as a kid I first heard the story about a great-uncle who was hit by lightning. He was bent over the engine of a stalled pickup truck at the edge of a field. I thought of lightning as a deadly finger tapping him on the shoulder as he cursed Ford Motor Company.

Like everything else, though, reality turns out to be more complicated. Lightning forks and dances about. Half the bolts hit the ground at more than one place.

I learned that after spending a week staring into trees and trying to figure the path of the lightning bolt that struck my house. I gave this up as an idle exercise. It seemed to have been everywhere all at once.

It hit the place like a bomb. Instead of experiencing the familiar, reassuring gap between seeing light and hearing thunder, I heard an explosion and instantaneously saw brilliant flashes, as though football stadium lights had been set up and were being switched on and off by pranksters outside the window. For the rest of the day the house smelled like a bumper-car ride.

I am no lightning wimp. I cannot be. I live in Central Florida, the Thunderstorm Capital of the Nation. For some reason, this designation is on no license plate, T-shirt, or bumper sticker I've found. Nowhere on Interstate 4 is a sign saying, "Welcome to Central Florida—The USA's Thunderstorm Capital."

I don't know why we're quiet about our awesome, busy skies. Our thunderstorms constitute a natural wonder. Not only in intensity but in number. We experience seventy to a hundred thunderstorm days a year.

"Come to Central Florida and watch the lightning strikes!" would be a dandy slogan targeting the more adventuresome traveler. Eco-tourists from places with tame, white-bread, boring old weather could come here to experience the full-bore natural drama of a ground-shaking, wind-making, Book of Revelations-style, day-turns-to-night-and-the-seas-boil-and-rage variety of thunderstorm. People ashamed of their lightning fears could come here to face them down.

These storms take my breath away every summer. Even when they aren't trying to burn my house down.

I eventually found the place where the lightning bolt struck. It hit a high-up limb of a large oak tree and left a narrow, blackened path of ripped bark as it sought the ground.

How the lightning moved from tree to downspout is unclear. But it baked and discolored the metal spout, popped its rivets, and tore it halfway off the house. Nearby it took two shallow scoops out of the driveway for good measure.

Was this the same bolt that burned the air conditioner, charred phone lines, baked the garage-door opener's circuitry to a golden brown, and escaped out the television cable, bursting insulation and popping connectors? That seemed like a lot of places for one rogue electrical charge to be. Was it more than one hit? Nobody could say.

"Lightning's funny," summed up one repair guy.

Nor was the mystery purely electrical.

"Maybe this is God punishing you," suggested my eighth-grade daughter.

"Maybe this is God warning you to get off the phone once in a while," I suggested right back.

Angry-deity theology is a game two can always play. And angry deities with lightning predate Christianity and the written word. We were engaged in speculation of a most ancient kind.

Regardless of your theology, there is something awe-inspiring and enlarging about having a billion volts of electricity visit one's house. Nature turbulent and random is no respecter of persons and places. We think we can make summer go away because we have air conditioning. Even though a summer lightning storm can dispatch an air-conditioning unit in an instant.

And sitting in the home without the telephone ringing, with the television and air conditioner disabled, I figured this was just as well. For the first time of the summer, I listened to tree frogs outside celebrating the damp.

June 1999

Tomokie must die!

The statue of Chief Tomokie in Tomoka State Park, Ormond Beach, is a public monument without peer. Good oddball public art is hard to find. Places sponsoring public sculpture tend to be overcautious and prone to bland abstraction or bombastic patriotism.

All the more reason to treasure the eccentric chief and to show him off a little. That's why I was touched when I read the Florida Senate had included $100,000 in this year's budget to fix him up.

"The Legend of Chief Tomokie" is one of two local monuments I often show visitors. The other is the Tomb of the Town Dog. ("BROWNIE/ THE TOWN DOG/ 1939–1954/ A GOOD DOG.")

Chief Tomokie statue, Tomoka State Park, Ormond Beach. (Photo by Mark Lane.)

The chief's monument is in much rougher shape Brownie's. Rising forty-five feet above a pool that would be reflecting if it held water, the chief suffers cracks, missing toes, exposed reinforcing rods, and other indignities. His spear fell off ages ago. And even when new, the work had a certain chunky, homecoming-parade-float feel to it. He is surrounded by a chain-link fence so kids won't go climbing around and inflicting art criticism on him.

This makes it hard when I bring people to see the Tomokie statute. I have to talk up his former greatness so they might see the true picture.

"The object you behold depicts the Native American legend of Chief Tomokie," I tell visitors when I'm in tour guide mode. It sounds even better when I can find batteries for the bullhorn. Sometimes I attract a crowd.

"The zaftig figure at the center of the edifice is the Indian maiden Oleeta, depicted in the act of skewering Tomokie with an arrow for the sacrilege of drinking the Water of Life from the Sacred Cup. (That's the object in Tomokie's hand shaped like a margarita glass.)

"Tomokie, rendered in reinforced concrete with brick powder, is the figure on top. In color and aspect, he resembles a fierce, primitive ancestor of Bert, back when Sesame Street was Sesame Forest.

"The robust, orange Amazon who slew him would, in turn, be killed with a poisoned arrow as she reclaimed the Sacred Cup.

"Like many of your finer Tales of Old Florida, someone had to go to a lot of effort to make this stuff up. Because the Native Americans who lived near this site all died out from disease in the eighteenth century, we know exactly nothing about any of the stories they might have told each other in their unwritten language.

"When asked about area native lore, local folks for more than a century simply shrugged and said 'beats me' or words to that effect.

"This made us sound ignorant and uninteresting to tourists until someone took the initiative to come up with something colorful in the 1950s. The artist Fred Dana Marsh fashioned this statue in 1957 to make the story seem even more authentic.

"This work of art celebrates more than just artificial folklore or just one community's practical joke. It is a monument to the Floridian tradition of making up stories to tell the tourists.

"Hey, you in back! What was that comment? That this statue looks like it was whupped with an ugly-stick? Well, very vividly expressed, Mr. Art Critic. I'll have you know that the Florida Senate sees $100,000 worth of beauty here. If you don't like our fake Indian mythology, make up your own."

"Any other questions?" I ask, staring them down.

Alas, I cannot send them away to the gift store because the park is short on Chief Tomokie paraphernalia. He would make a great key chain, scary mask, or snowing paperweight, if any entrepreneur would make the effort. A "Tomokie Must Die!" T-shirt would be very cool and help pay for restoration.

Some people find the concrete chief ghastly, misshapen, politically incorrect, and embarrassing. Some say that although Marsh was a talented artist, reinforced concrete just wasn't his medium. Valid viewpoints I'm sure, but I guarantee you won't find anything similar anywhere else. Even in Vegas. And on a coastline dotted with towns as indistinguishable as interstate exits, it sometimes takes an extreme aesthetic statement to prove we're different from everywhere else.

Which is why Florida should support our local concrete chief.

May 1999

Postscript: Time has not been kind to Chief Tomokie. Governor Jeb Bush ve-toed the restoration money in 1999. In 2002 two tourists vandalized the statue and ran off with Oleeta's head.

Shark Attack Summer

"Ocean Temp: 78. Surf: Gnarly." That's what the chalkboard sign on the lifeguard tower said. "Gnarly" is more usually rendered "rough" on the tower signs, but I appreciated the writer's enthusiasm.

I was out bodysurfing until the lightning storms got too close and melodramatic. I like to say "bodysurfing" because it sounds so fit, so active when compared to the alternative. Which is to say I was "floating around in the surf and letting the waves wash me to shore to avoid the effort of swimming back in."

And the beach last weekend had great bodysurfing conditions. Also, as most of the English-speaking, cable-television–watching, and Internet-connected world knows, it also had great shark conditions. Great from the sharks's point of view, I mean.

The unusual number of shark nips, nibbles, and bites—let's please dispense with the alarmist phrase "shark attack"—has folks worried this summer. It's good to be noticed, but this is not the kind of global publicity a tourist destination generally seeks.

And it's a story that just keeps swimming along. We think it will die if it stops moving forward, but that's just a myth.

Tales of surfers hopping over sharks to get out to the waves have appeared in the *New York Times* and the *Wall Street Journal*. Pictures of bandaged surfers have appeared in the *National Post* in Canada (a country where, it should be remembered, bear repellant enjoys brisk sales). You can click on shark images online or wait a half hour and see the shark segment again on *CNN Headline News*.

Shark Attack Summer has reached the point that calls from out of town are coming in. Any longtime Florida resident knows this kind of out-of-town phone call. We got them three years ago during the wildfires. *Just calling to make sure you haven't been incinerated.* We got them during the last busy hurricane season. *Just making sure you aren't under water.* Now: *just calling to make sure you haven't been bitten by sharks.*

"Naw, no more than most summers," I say.

Actually, I enjoy these inquiries. They allow me to maintain the exciting fiction that Florida is an exotic place fraught with daily danger.

In a county of 443,000 residents and millions of tourists, twenty people have been bitten by sharks this year. While that ruined the days of all twenty people, it is not a massive public health danger.

As potentially lethal beach perils go, skin cancer should rank higher. Yet many viewers of cable news think we are an area under aquatic attack. That "Closed Until Shark Bites Heal" signs hang from business doorknobs and that the town has more one-legged people than a bad pirate movie.

So what is to be done?

Well, downplaying things won't help. Somehow when you try to put things in perspective, it only sounds worse. Pointing out that most of the sharks involved were such *small* sharks. That they don't mean to bite people. That some of these were pokes and nibbles rather than bites per se. That you're more likely to be hit by lightning. . . . It all sounds as though we don't take the brutal, man-eating horrors of the deep seriously.

Instead, many have taken the proverbial lemon and made metaphorical lemonade. Already, "shark-bite capital of the world" T-shirts are popping up in tourist shops. This is a healthy response. It gives tourists a vicarious sense of danger. They can wander the beach, then go home and answer questions from interested neighbors who saw scary things on TV.

Tourists fly all over the world seeking exciting and interesting places. Places other people might actually want to hear about.

I recommend the county put up "gnarly" warning signs with sharks eating pedestrian crossing–style stick figures. Tourists love to be photographed next to scary warning signs. Like the moose-warning signs in New Hampshire and mountain lion–warning signs out West.

If we just play up the danger a little longer and a little bigger, we could be that kind of destination. An exotic place where nature fights back. Not some paper-umbrella-in-a-coconut-cup resort. A place for those who dare to live rich, exciting lives. Lives of danger and excitement!

The rest would sell itself.

August 2001

Guys in shades

In most pictures of me taken when I was a kid I wear the same expression: eyes narrowed into slits, nose slightly wrinkled. In most pictures of me taken as an adult my expression is a cipher: the guy in the shades. If eyes are the windows to the soul, mine are no more than peepholes.

Having grown up under brilliant white-blue Florida skies, there is an extensive collection of wavy-edged, black-and-white photos of me standing in front of signs advertising the state's preeminent second-tier, pre-Disney tourist attractions while reacting to the glare of the subtropical sun. Or sitting on boat cushions with light bouncing from the pellucid water into my nearly shut eyes. Or hands blurred in front of face fending off flash-bulb explosions like an actor waving off paparazzi. My childhood memories seem strangely overexposed.

It was not until I was an adult that a helpful eye doctor told me, almost as an aside, that I have this condition whereby my pupils overdilate in bright light. Suddenly my whole squinty past made sense.

This knowledge was welcome but came far too late to do much good, for this physiological quirk had already shaped me in surprising ways. Walking around with dilated pupils and half-closed eyes had a way of making me look shifty as a kid and stoned as a young adult. This made authorities react to me in predictable ways. This, in turn, gave me a rather predictable attitude toward authority. On the bright side—very bright—it prepared me admirably for journalism, a profession in which you regularly walk into rooms where everybody distrusts you on sight.

These days I wear shades everywhere, all the time. Cloudy days. Sometimes indoors. Really dark ones, too. Wraparounds when I'm doing something active. Blues Brothers–style glasses for hanging out. My ex-wife made me get rid of the mirrored aviator glasses. She said they creeped her out.

This collection represents a vast improvement over my unfocused past. Plus, it's a look that tells the world, "Hey, you don't know that I'm incredibly nearsighted; maybe I just wear these because I want to wear them. Maybe I'm just one of those people who feel this part of their Florida identity."

And this presents its own social drawbacks. People see a guy in shades indoors or on an overcast day and they think you're an over-optimistic tourist, a wannabe hipster, somebody who must think he's too cool for the frozen-food aisle, a celebrity in his own mind, somebody nursing a hangover.

Dark shades are associated with out-of-work musicians, Old Guys with Some Sort of Condition, junkies in anti-drug pamphlets, newcomers who bought into the Florida thing a little too intensely using material they gathered from TV.

And to be sure, the flashiness of my shades clashes violently with my personal style of dress, which I describe as Coastal Casual but has been less charitably characterized as "Tropical Goodwill" or "The Grad Student on the Beach Look."

No matter. I endured discomfort and the silent censure of society as a squinty little kid. I'll do the same in comfort as the guy who strides the dairy aisle in superdark prescription Ray-Bans.

Besides, people don't mess with a guy in these kind of glasses. There's no telling what dark thoughts he is thinking.

June 2006

Gold, monsters, and second-place danger

Danger is my middle name. Well, actually, Robert is my middle name. But if middle names really and truly meant something, then danger might be my informal middle name with quote marks because I live in Florida.

Florida has been certified as a Genuine Dangerous Place by widely quoted experts. Morgan Quinto Press, which does all sorts of state-by-state comparisons, last week declared Florida the second most dangerous state in the union. Up from third place last year and fourth the year before.

Nevada was named number one for danger, but I'm not worried. The most endangered thing in Nevada is its top billing. But even at number two, Florida has a finer quality of personal danger. This state stands for regular, consistent, year-in-and-year-out danger. Dependable danger. Nevada, in contrast, is into flashy, here-today, gone-tomorrow danger.

Plus, because Florida is a Caribbean crossroads and not off in a desert somewhere near a bunch of big, bland, and chunky square states, we have more cosmopolitan, exotic, and international dangers than Nevada. If quality and variety of criminal behavior counted more than mere quantity, Florida would be number one.

Naturally state tourism officials are expressing concern about the effects this designation might have on the state. They worry that a number two designation could scare away the faint- hearted while not being dangerous enough to encourage danger tourism.

And they have good reasons to be annoyed. Is a designation that only takes into account criminal activity a fair indicator of danger when there are other, really fine dangers that the state can brag about? I think not.

Central Florida is the lightning-strike capital of America, but did that get factored into this rating? Uh-uh. Dangerous mutant animal life? No again. Poisonous plants? Snakes and alligators and spiders the size of Frisbees? Just not dangerous enough to make the list.

Earlier in the year, Florida cities gained top national mention for being dangerous to both bicycle riders and pedestrians. Did that get us bonus points? No again.

Was this state's per-capita rating of people using heavy machinery while taking sinus pills factored in? Nope. And what about the state's remarkable ratio of elderly drivers who view the road from under the steering wheel per mile of state four-lane highway? Another vital statistic overlooked.

This is even worse because Florida displays a certain regional pride in being dangerous. Other top ten states whine about it and quibble about methodology. Floridians who know that growth management begins at home already are calling their relatives. Other states feel put upon. We feel affirmed.

Scaring the tourists is a Florida tradition as rich and ancient as land fraud. It dates from dim ages past when Indians alternated between telling Spanish explorers about gold and about monsters.

We are no more consistent now. We tell people this is Disney's hometown America—but watch out because people sometimes machine-gun each other when traffic backs up. That this is a sunny, near-tropical near-paradise—except for the hurricanes, trailer-seeking tornadoes, and Old Testament–intensity thunderstorms that fry golfers and can send your cat under the sofa all summer. That we are a carefree outdoor playground—except when large reptiles crawl out to eat people. That we are a verdant land of natural wonder—except for the parts that have been drained, paved over, subdivided, pushed to the brink of ecological collapse, or are on fire at the moment.

Gold and monsters—they've sold the place from time immemorial. If it worked any better, we'd be dangerous. Oh right, I suppose we are.

July 1997

Danger: Photo op ahead!

A friend of mine sent me photos from her travels out West—a big square state with lots of sand, I forget which one. The snapshots had the three items of proof one demands of anyone claiming to have had a rugged old time in such locales—a mountain, cactus, and warning signs.

She did this because she understood my enthusiasm for warning-sign travel photography. Next to photographing giant animals made of fiberglass or cement, they are my favorite on-the-road photographic subjects.

A good warning sign in a snapshot marks you as an intrepid traveler. The more exotic the danger, the more points you get.

One of her signs said, "DANGER / HIGH MOUNTAIN / LION ACTIVITY / ENTER AT YOUR OWN RISK." This has everything one wants in a hiking photo. And the quicksand warning posted next to it made it almost too perfect. Still, I have quibbles.

First: no pictograph. Everybody loves the wordless adventures of the little dot-and-line man shown on warning signs. To see him hit by lightning. Doing something unwise with a circle around him and a line through him. Or lying prostrate after doing something dumb.

Dot-and-line man is the Wile E. Coyote of the warning-sign maker's art. I'm always anxious to see the next exotic peril awaiting him.

Second: I read this sign as saying "Danger: High mountain! Lion activity! Enter at your own risk." Which turns out to be wrong. And I hate to nitpick, but a mountain is not something one enters. (Unless, of course, there's an ancient secret tunnel carved into it, as in *Lord of the Rings*.)

I would reword this "Danger: / Mountain lions live here. / They might eat you! / Have a nice day." This conveys peril, a sense of place, and sends you on your way. Everything a tourist wishes for in a warning sign. (Except for a dot-and-line man being eaten.)

When I wish to let people know I live in a place of unpredictable danger—which is often and easy to do because I live in Florida—I try to casually include photos of local versions of such signs. Like the standard-issue state-park alligator-warning signs.

They have a picture of dot-and-line man swimming with a circle and line over his oblivious body. Below him is a grinning green alligator with teeth like a tree saw.

"CAUTION! / ALLIGATORS / NO SWIMMING," it says.

I like the use of the word *caution*. It's a step down from the alarmist *danger* or harsh *warning*. *Caution* suggests we need not get all jumpy. This is normal. Just keep your head about you.

In smaller letters it says "WE ARE CONCERNED ABOUT WILDLIFE" and "WE ARE CONCERNED ABOUT PEOPLE." This strikes me as oddly defensive. As though the park folks want us to understand that in erecting this sign, they are not actually taking sides between alligators and people. The state of Florida is concerned about us both.

When a Florida tourist is deprived of seeing an alligator, an alligator-warning sign is the next best thing. I have more than once been asked to photograph smiling tourists next to one. The sign, I mean.

In a world of packaged tours, don't-leave-the-walkway parks, and formerly exotic places overrun with travelers, the signage can be the only hint in the visual record that we've been anywhere interesting. I suspect many places realize this and put up unnecessary warnings to delight tourists. That is why, for instance, there are more moose-warning signs than moose in New England.

Maybe. But that doesn't dim my enthusiasm. I expect more and scarier signage each time I travel. And I'm seldom disappointed.

November 2004

Who belongs here? Let's tally points

I got an e-mail from an acquaintance in France who said that while she never lived in Florida, she did ride out a hurricane in Key West and felt that that should count for something more than average by way of an Authentic Florida Experience.

Indeed it does, Mademoiselle. I assured her she owned many valuable Florida points and should feel free to elaborate on the story with gusto.

In terms of having a story to tell and being able to impart a little local color, a day of hurricane-strength winds on Duval Street is more than the experiential equivalent of, say, living in Longwood for eight months, deciding it's too hot, and moving back to Paramus.

The more I thought about it, the more I liked the whole Florida points concept. Remember: the vast majority of people here are from somewhere else. Except for the tiny number of natives, everyone is only relatively a Floridian. A Floridian compared to those folks who only came lately and never immersed themselves in the Florida-ness of their new homes.

This is in stark contrast to a place like New Hampshire, where only a second-generation Hampshirite can claim his or her first New Hampshire point. Here we generously throw out points. In a single year you can garner enough Florida-experience points to laugh at tourists.

Riding out a hurricane is a good example. This is a quintessential Florida experience. One even a Parisian can turn in for Florida points. It won't gain you crackerhood, but it will give you a cultural toehold.

I imagine the system would be something like this:

Hearing about a hurricane on the Weather Channel, driving north on I-95, and gravely watching it on TV in a Motel 8 in Valdosta, Georgia—one point.

Hearing about a hurricane, nailing up the same plywood you nailed up last year, standing in line behind people doing pre-hurricane panic buying, then staying at home until the evacuation is declared—two points.

Hearing about a hurricane, nailing up the plywood you nailed up for the past four years, staying home until someone in a uniform tells you the evacuation was yesterday—three points.

As above and staying anyway—four points.

As above and being located by paramedics a few days later—ten points.

In this continuum, watching pool furniture blow past your hotel window on Duval Street and wondering if Key West is the kind of place that regularly slips under the sea merits three points. At least.

But Florida is not just about dangerous natural disasters. It's about dangerous animals, too.

If you've made any of the following statements you gain points:

"Is it 'red touches yellow/can kill a fellow,' or 'red against yellow/just stay mellow?' I never can remember that damn rhyme, particularly when I see one that size and it starts acting all nervous."

"But they're just small sharks."

"Any roach smaller than a shoebox isn't worth digging out the spray for."

"Just put meat tenderizer on it and the stinging will stop."

Growing up in Florida gets intense Florida points because those are formative years and they make you a living link to a vanishing landscape. Points are freely granted if you have pictures of yourself as a small kid standing next to the coquina Marineland sign, standing next to a building shaped like a giant orange or a giant alligator. Points, too, for pictures of yourself holding any large dead fish, large dead snake, large dead okra. Heck, any dead thing longer than you. And points for knowing where the edge of town used to be.

You get points, too, if you get nostalgic on seeing beige portable classrooms. Extra points, too, if, when asked in class for an example of a homonym, you said, "racing" and "raisin."

Oh, and points if you read to the end of a newspaper column speculating on the right of even French people to tell Florida stories. Lots of points. I see this system as working for everyone.

May 2002

Halfbacks flee summer

Summer should not be a surprise. Even in August. Even in Florida. Yet each year summer shock seems to fuel the halfback phenomenon.

"Halfbacks" are people who come down to Florida, live here a bit, turn around, and move halfway back. They are a demographic construct. A composite character to explain the numbers. And the numbers say that roughly a third of the people who come to Florida change their mind at some point and turn around. A few of them go home, but most of them seem to go somewhere in between. The Carolinas and Georgia mostly.

Why? Heat and humidity combine with a creeping feeling that this is not a Normal Place to make faint-hearted newcomers rethink their commitment to the Sunshine State Dream. There are lots of theories. Sadly, nobody from the Census Bureau asked those who packed their bags whether it was something we said.

Some say traffic and taxes are factors. I doubt this. Nobody coming here from New York can complain about taxes or traffic. Not with a straight face.

I would hasten to add that this is not said out of anti–New York animus. I have friends who are New Yorkers. Florida, moreover, is a place where New Yorkers are considered a distinct ethnic group with its own colorful contributions to local culture. After a few years here they mutate into that familiar local hyphenate, the NY-Floridian.

The true NY-Floridian is not fazed because cars are blocking his way or the Water Management District increased property taxes by $2.95 a year. He considers his new neighbors tax-wimps and traffic-wimps. He's seen worse and would be only too happy to share those memories with you.

This certain knowledge that things are impressively worse elsewhere makes the NY-Floridian, for all his grousing, a tolerably good sport. Taxes, traffic, and new neighbors who ride motorcycles and sacrifice chickens in the backyard to barbarous and unspeakable gods are all matters to be taken in stride.

Move to Carolina over that? Whaddayahnuts?

That leaves summer shock as the only possible motivation for halfbackery.

Some people say summer begins on Memorial Day. Some people say it begins when school lets out. Purists point to the summer solstice. But the real first day of Florida summer is a physical sensation.

It arrives the day you walk outside and the thick, humid air envelops you as though some prankster dropped a warm, moist blanket over your head. The day your glasses steam up upon opening the car door. The day you mow only half the lawn. The day when complaining about the heat seems like too much effort, and you're reduced to whining telepathically.

It's the day that turns an almost-naturalized Floridian into a halfback, snowbird, or refugee. Anecdotal evidence abounds.

Why this surprises anybody is beyond me. Yes, it's hot here. Look on a map. Trace a line with your finger from the Sahara Desert across the blue and see where you're pointing. That's right, the Sunshine State. We share a latitude with some of the most unappealing places on the planet. Funny how that works out.

People who carefully plan the details of their Florida retirement arrive to discover that August brings an entirely different kind of hot than they imagined or even have a vocabulary for. An un-American kind of hot. The kind of heat you'd expect in a place with a methane atmosphere.

Well good riddance, halfbacks. Don't let the screen door hit you on the way out. Florida isn't for weather wimps. Next trip, consult a map and an almanac.

The trick to enjoying Florida summer is simply to understand that personal energy is a finite resource. Something that should not be squandered on trifles or be taken for granted. Use it more sparingly in August and invest $10 in a second pair of flip-flops for more formal occasions and you're halfway there. This is an attitude that not only gets you through summer but can color your outlook through the rest of the year and, perhaps, your life.

People who don't appreciate these techniques will not be helped by fleeing to Georgia. But that might be a good first step.

June 1997

Snow in Florida is beyond words

Any temperature with the number two in front of it is a troubling experience for a Floridian. It challenges your wardrobe, your vocabulary, your sense of reality. And nobody from out of state feels your pain.

First off, it's a damp cold, okay. This is not your crisp, energizing cold. This is swamp cold. It's different. It's bad.

Now, note that last sentence again. It's bad. That's what people are reduced to saying when this kind of meteorological record is broken. A normally voluble people who can summon any one of two hundred commonly used figures of speech, metaphors, and old jokes to describe the heat of August were reduced to saying things like, "it's bad" and "Woo, it's really cold out there" to describe the weather last week. Pathetic.

"How cold is it?" my daughter asked as I came in from walking the dog in the morning. She was frowning because it was beginning to look as though she'd have to wear a sweater and coat to school, a combination that no matter how svelte one is, rather harms a silhouette.

"It's so cold . . ." I began.

So cold what?

"So cold . . . so cold I thought I'd freeze out there," I declared.

"It's bad," I added. For emphasis.

Yeah, I know. I'm a professional communicator and that's the best I could do. But this was all just too far outside of all my usual frames of reference.

And then it snowed. Not a big, get-out-the-toboggan snow. "Flurry" was the word some used to describe it, but that was an exaggeration. I squinted, looked hard at the sky, and saw a few tiny specks blown about by the wind. Specks that seemed to correspond in some way to descriptions of snow I'd encountered in literature and in Christmas carols.

"Wow, snow," I observed.

"It's bad out here," I quickly added.

I ran over to trudge through it—which all my reading tells me is what one does through snow—but the flakes melted before I could get to them.

"I can't believe I have to go to school *through the snow*," my daughter said indignantly, frowning at the single pin-dot of moisture on the driveway. Indeed, school had been canceled in Flagler County, just north of us, because of cold. There was a freeze, after all.

People above forty degrees north latitude find these reactions hilarious.

"They let out school because somebody saw a snowflake and the high was in the forties?" a representative voice of the far north asked me over the phone. And not in a sympathetic tone of voice, either. She was clearly not sharing our pain. I quickly added that it was very damp and breezy, too, and that it was bad out there.

Word of the nearby school holiday only contributed to a general holiday feel to the day. A bona fide below-freezing day in Florida is like Halloween. A day when expectations are overturned and people dress up in funny, exaggerated, and exotic clothing.

They wear hats. They wear the coat that had been in storage ever since it had been packed for the moving van. They unwrap the scarves and sweaters sent as Christmas presents from distant relatives who have no idea what the climate is like here.

They dress up in their best approximation of somebody from out of town. Some more authentically than others.

How cold was it? Glad you asked. So cold I wore shoes on a weekend. Both days. No exaggeration.

It was that bad out there.

January 2003

Bones and past lurk under sidewalks

I sometimes wonder why land development in Florida is so often bigger, uglier, more ambitious, and less fettered by law, economics, local planning, or public sentiment than in most places. I suspect it's because Florida's big natural spaces have always invited the idea that this is a place where you can build from scratch, answerable neither to nature nor history. There's just so much of the former here and so little of the latter, it's tempting to think that nothing under a bulldozer's treads will be missed.

It's an attitude that encourages places that are wildly out of place with their surroundings. Italian villas in the hammock. Ye Olde Tudor houses on barrier islands. And the suburbs of midwestern industrial cities reproduced in loving detail where orange groves used to be.

When you're working on a blank slate, there's no need to pay attention to anything around you. For this reason, any time nature or the past asserts itself I'm delighted to hear about it.

Usually nature does the asserting. Woods on fire in the early summer. Hurricanes in the late summer. Sinkholes year-round. Poodle-eating reptiles wandering into subdivision canals.

History asserts itself rarely. But it can on occasion. Like last week when a skull was discovered at a construction site in downtown Daytona Beach. Under a sidewalk. In an older part of a youngish town. Across the street from the old A&P grocery market. Near the '40s-era drugstore malt shop.

This being Florida, bodies have a way of turning up with alarming frequency for backhoe operators, and one does tend to call a cop rather than an archaeologist. But looking it over, the Medical Examiner's Office gave Downtown Skull to archaeologists who pronounced it at least seventy-five years old, likely older.

The guess is Downtown Skull Person was a member of the long-extinct Timucuan tribe. But who knows?

That some kind of native people lived in this neighborhood is well-known. Probably Timucuans, but maybe some stray Aias wandered a little north. Perhaps as a prank to mess up archaeological maps.

When Daytona was founded in 1876 there were two large shell mounds in the area. One was near the present-day Fifth District Court of Appeal courthouse. The other near the Seabreeze Bridge.

Before we had high-rise bridges these were the best places in town to climb up for a view of the place. Which by all accounts was a popular thing to do.

The residents appreciated the Indian mounds. They made excellent road-building material. So excellent, there is no hint of them now. Not even a bump in the ground.

The skull did not become a stop-everything kind of find. There were no signs of any unusual sacred site, like the ceremonial circle found in downtown Miami in 1998, or a burial mound full of people's bones, like the mound south of the library in Ormond Beach. Just a stray head.

Downtown Skull will be given to native people for burial, which I suppose is more dignified than being under a sidewalk. Still, I'd like to think there's something to be said for staying in your hometown. Next to a road constructed, at least in its lower strata, from shellfish your family ate.

Requiescat in pace, Downtown Skull Person. You remind us that this place is not as brand new as it looks. And if we think it exists only for us, right now, well, so did you and the other shellfish eaters.

And that you never know what, or whom, you're walking over.

November 2005

Hey, tourist, heed your nation's call!

In the aftermath of the fires that have incinerated much of Florida's pine forests this summer, we have been hosts to a parade of dignitaries. People we seldom saw in the, uh, beforemath of the fires.

The president himself showed up and was a great hit. Bill Clinton shook hands with firefighters, listened to fire victims, and was sympathetic to local officials even when they started to get all whiny. He was in town only for a few hours, but he felt everyone's pain as fast as humanly possible before zipping into the sky for the next fundraiser. But he particularly warmed local hearts when he got on television and reminded people around the world that despite the fire, Florida is still open for business.

"If you haven't taken your vacation yet, and you want to know where to come, give the people in this area an economic boost," Clinton said.

Here was the bully pulpit of the presidency being mobilized for the noble cause of telling Americans to roll up their sleeves, do their patriotic duty, and go to the beach.

It brought tears to my eyes. But after weeks of smoke, that's been happening a lot.

The notion that tourism can be a form of volunteerism deserves greater national attention and official encouragement. It's a rare and exemplary citizen who is willing to drop his or her daily concerns, pack a bathing suit, and go to Florida.

These brave volunteers are willing to rush to tourist-deprived areas, book rooms, eat out, and tip 20 percent. And their sacrifices are too often overlooked.

It was well that the president took the time to urge volunteer tourists to undertake new such humanitarian missions. Sadly, though, mere exhortation isn't always enough.

When natural disasters strike Florida and other tourism centers, they need more help than an unpredictable stream of freelance tourists can give. They need something more dependable. More organized. They need the National Tourism Corps.

Tour Corps, as it might be popularly called, would be an elite organization of highly trained tourists ready at a moment's notice to vacation where the need is greatest. Modeled after the National Guard, the Peace Corps, and Club Med, these citizen-travelers would be excused from work to hang out, spend money, and tip the locals 20 percent in federally designated tourist-deprived zones. After the first wave of firefighters, paramedics, National Guard, and news media on expense accounts leave town, Tour Corps would be flown in to take their places and make sure the beaches in a disaster area never empty and the bars keep running.

Immediately recognizable in their government-issue Hawaiian shirts, the corps would have a large number of general, family-type tourists but would also include a number of highly trained specialists. Special-forces tourists like scuba divers, surf dudes, boaters, Jetskiers, bikers, bicyclists, recreational shoppers, gourmands, theatergoers, thrill-ride enthusiasts, music-lovers, and bar-hoppers would be airlifted to devastated areas that depend on particular niche-tourism markets.

Unfortunately the Tour Corps idea remains unrealized. The plan languishes, unable to gain a hearing before a small-minded Congress that doesn't understand the plight of tourist-dependent areas.

Maybe this is too big for Congress. We are living in a global economic system, and Florida has the same problems as other tourist-dependent economies of the Caribbean. Maybe the United Nations should take up the challenge and form a multinational tourist force ready to spend top dollar for rooms in blighted tourist spots around the globe. They could hit the beaches after island hurricanes, keep restaurants open after the war correspondents leave, and see the pyramids soon after terrorist attacks.

In the meantime, though, we must be content with voluntary half-measures and hope that you, the caring citizens of a great nation, will listen to your president, do your duty, and fly down here to spend money.

And don't forget to go back home when you're done.

July 1998

There's no noir like Sunshine State Noir

This has been a good month for local fans of the Sunshine State Noir school of novel writing. Tim Dorsey was here twice and S. V. Dáte gave a talk Wednesday.

Dorsey's latest book, *The Big Bamboo*, came out last month. Dáte's last book was *Quiet Passion*, a decidedly nonfiction biography of Bob Graham, but among less–politically inclined people, he's known for novels like *Deep Water* and *Speed Week*. The latter is set in the World's Most Famous Beach and is an excellent gift for anyone who needs to think twice before moving here.

Sunshine State Noir is Florida's only homegrown literary school. Its founding father is John D. MacDonald. It came of age with Elmore Leonard. Its preeminent practitioner right now is Carl Hiaasen. (No writer of Sunshine State Noir is officially part of the movement until Hiaasen bestows a book-jacket blurb.)

Some critical readers will object. These are not serious works. These books are airplane and beach reading. They have raised letters on their covers. Are you calling these production-line mysteries a movement, a school, a literary subgenre?

You bet. Just as Florida's lasting contribution to architecture has been hotel design, its contribution to literature is breathing life into the creaky mechanics of the mystery novel.

There are a lot of mystery novels set in Florida, but not all of them qualify as Sunshine State Noir. To be Sunshine State Noir novels they must present Florida as a deeply weird place populated by virtuous and colorful locals, crooked and colorful politicians, megalomaniacal land developers (colorful or not), criminal transients, and dangerous reptiles.

It helps if there are crooked but folksy politicians with a fondness for aphorisms, Weeki Wachee mermaids gone to seed, ageless old guys whose fatalism is leavened with mystical insights, and surf dudes whose mystical insights are leavened with dangerous chemicals. They must have a main character who lands in Florida from harsher climes seeking a freer, mellower life and some kind of vague personal healing but instead finds More Than He Bargained For.

One figure you won't find in a Sunshine State Noir novel: the criminal genius. If there's a criminal genius in a book, it's not a Sunshine State

Noir novel. We do not have criminal geniuses here. And not because we lack a lively, on-the-go criminal population, either. I blame chronic school underfunding.

I'm a big fan of Sunshine State Noir. It convinces me that I live in a bigger-than-life place amid natural splendor, political squalor, and thoroughgoing societal weirdness.

And, as Dáte and Dorsey show, it's a literary school that provides work for reporters. And not just crime reporters, legislative reporters.

These are not stories ripped from the front page. These are stories lifted from the inside Local/State pages. Which are usually more interesting.

In *Black Sunshine*, Dáte kills off a thinly disguised Bob Milligan in the first chapter. In how many other states would a state comptroller be fodder for fiction? Only in Florida do political wonks regularly turn to crime novels.

Most of all, I love Sunshine State Noir because of the theme inherent in the mayhem, deviant psychology, and cheap jokes. The theme is this: Florida is an unearthly beautiful place being destroyed by forces beyond the control of the inhabitants. These must be dark forces or they wouldn't be wrecking such a place. Listen, here's a story to show how dark these forces are and reassure you they don't always win . . .

This story, told over and over, has, like any great regional mythology, deep, not always articulated explanatory powers. Powers that make strange events seem psychologically right. That give a kind of order to the closer precincts of the universe. And celebrate why we're like that.

May 2006

Index

Mark Lane is a metro columnist for the *Daytona Beach News-Journal,* where he has worked as a reporter, editorial writer, rim guy, and copy boy. His columns have appeared in newspapers nationally. He lives in Ormond Beach.